SALMON RIVER'S END

*Tragedies on the Lower Columbia River
in the 1870s, 1880s, and 1890s.*

**Articles from Astoria newspapers
Collected by Liisa Penner**

*This picture was taken at the Union Fisherman's Dock in Astoria, Oregon in
about 1910. Left to right • Salmon weights 116 lbs and 121 lbs. They were
salted down in 100 lb barrels and sent to Europe on sailing ships.*

[Original picture caption.]

SALMON FEVER: RIVER'S END

*Tragedies on the Lower Columbia River
in the 1870s, 1880s, and 1890s.*

**Articles from Astoria newspapers
Collected by Liisa Penner**

Frank Amato
PORTLAND

Photographs and map courtesy Clatsop County Historical Society. Photograph numbers in order as they appear in the color section: 5698-315; 15,347-350; 4417-320; 12,868-320; 3908-315; 277-315; 4255-315; 7145-320; 21,050-315; 5393-315; 8921-315; 275-315; 3861-320.

Cannery Labels from Frank Amato personal collection

Published in 2006 by
Frank Amato Publications, Inc.
PO Box 82112 • Portland, Oregon 97282 • (503) 653-8108
Softbound ISBN: 1-57188-390-8 • Softbound UPC: 0-81127-00224-5

Book Design: Leslie Brannan
Printed in Hong Kong

1 3 5 7 9 10 8 6 4 2

CONTENTS

Chinook Salmon
Weight From
60 to 74 lbs Each

Kinney's Cannery

1886

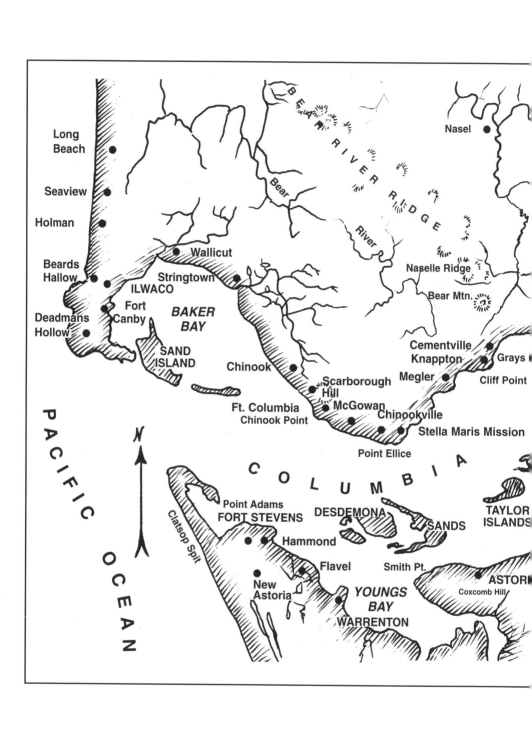

Map Circa 1900

One inch equals about two and a quarter miles.

Durten Kampmann map based on a map by Liisa Penner.

SALMON FEVER: RIVER'S END

*Tragedies on the Lower Columbia River
in the 1870s, 1880s, and 1890s.*

**Articles from Astoria newspapers
Collected by Liisa Penner**

The water at the mouth of the Columbia River is cold. Temperatures range from the forties in winter to the sixties in summer (Fahrenheit). For the man who falls off a boat into the water now, the experience is frightening and miserable, but help is usually soon on the way. Lightweight clothing, life jackets and flotation devices keep him buoyant while the radio on board his boat sends out distress calls to the Coast Guard who dispatch helicopters and boats to locate and pluck him out of the water.

No radios or helicopters or boats of the modern Coast Guard rescued the man who was thrown overboard in the 1800s. Few ever survived. Heavy clothing, quickly water-soaked, pulled the victims under the surface before anyone nearby could help. Some managed to float for a while, waves slapping against their faces, the cold paralyzing their limbs, their weakening cries for help going unheeded or unheard until they too sank down into the water.

How dangerous was it to work on the river in the 1870s, 1880s, and 1890s? The following articles from the Astoria newspapers reveal a past many have forgotten or may have never known. The articles that appear here are only a small portion of the total number.

Abbreviations of the names of local newspapers

ADB	Astoria Daily Budget
DA	Daily Astorian
DMA	Daily Morning Astorian *(sometimes written as DA)*
MA	Morning Astorian
TWA	Tri-Weekly Astorian
WA	Weekly Astorian

Articles in the DA and DMA often show up in the WA.

THE
1870'S

November 29, 1873

THE COLUMBIA RIVER SALMON FISHERIES
Written for the TRI-WEEKLY ASTORIAN

WASHINGTON IRVING, in his much read *Astoria*, related the manner of taking the Salmon of the Columbia river by the natives, before the devices of civilization and science encroached upon the pristine method. At that time many Indians lived along the river subsisting mainly upon the fish, taken from its clear waters, and exchanging their surplus catches with interior tribes for hides and land game.

When the pioneers came upon the river, they secured and preserved the fish for their own use, but as the settlers became more numerous and commerce began to grow, the new comers likewise engaged in the traffic of the salmon until now the catch amounts to about one million dollars in coin per year.

The Custom-house records at Astoria show that there were shipped from the Columbia river during the year ending October 31st, 1873, the following amounts of Salmon:

To Liverpool, 3,000 cases and 200 kits;

To China, 1,500 cases and 63 barrels;
To Melbourne, Australia, 475 cases;

To Honolulu, 20 cwt, smoked, 1,512 barrels,
267 half barrels, 30 quarter barrels, 151 kits and 77 cases;

To Port Townsend, 287 packages, and 20 kits;

To San Francisco, 68,890 cases, 7,961 packages,
189 tierces, 2798 barrels, 1,738 half barrels, 119 quarter barrels
and 101 kits;

Amounting in value to about $700,000.

The quantity and manner of curing of the packages are unknown, but the cases are of canned, and the barrels, kits, etc., of pickled or salted Salmon. This statement does not include all that has been carried to sea from the river, because some of the sailing coast vessels do not report at the Custom-house. There is not included the amounts also consumed by the States and Territories bordering on the river, so that we think the number taken during the past season can safely be estimated at 500,000 of a value of $1,000,000.

The Columbia river Salmon are said to be the best on this coast. In the waters north of here are fabulous quantities of plump fish, but they are considered less finely flavored, though few, perhaps, could distinguish them apart on the table. The fish here average twelve pounds each, net, but of the number there is no counting them. In April they enter the river, and continue to do so until August, pushing their way up stream, leaping rapids and floundering on shoals, to the head waters of the Columbia and its tributaries.

Though many persons think the supply inexhaustible, the history of depleted rivers on the Atlantic coast, and the present scarcity of the fish in the Sacramento, admonish us to not rest too confidently in the opinion of the many, but to encourage the growth of the fish in our river. Many fish destroy themselves trying to leap the rapids on the vogage to the spawning grounds. It has been ascertained, by actual experiment, that the Salmon after entering and living for a season in the ocean, return to the same streams in which they began life. The greater, then, the number produced in any stream, the greater will be the "run" in the future fishing seasons. There should, wherever practicable, be placed fish ladders or other means by which the transit of the fish over the falls of the rapids would be facilitated. There is one place deserving of especial attention, the Wallamet falls...

The catch next year, if the "run" should be as good as the last, will reach over one million fish, and the business increasing one hundred per cent. Immense, indeed is the supply that cannot be exhausted at that rate. If there should be fish enough, the business of preserving them will continue to increase as long as the market does. The market for pickled salmon was confined, before the Continental railway, chiefly to Honolulu and home demands. The fish would not bear shipment through [long voyages], but with the completion of the railway, the market was extended, not only for pickled but also for fresh Salmon. By packing in ice the fish can be taken by the car load from the Sacramento to New York fresh, where they bring as high as one dollar per pound. It will be years before the culture of the Salmon in the Atlantic slope can limit the market there, notwithstanding the large sums of money being expended in its behalf. But preserving the fish in cans, as meats and vegetables are preserved, opened the whole world as a market. When the canning was commenced on the Columbia river five years since, it was difficult to effect sales of fish so preserved. Purchasers had to be solicited, and consumers made acquainted, with the novelty. This year, however, orders were received from Europe before the first fish could be taken, one firm having an order ahead for 15,000 cases. All the fisheries have been able to realize as fast as the Salmon could be placed on board ship, and no longer will canners have to beg of the people to taste an unknown dish.

Catching the fish on the upper Columbia was formerly done by half-naked savages, standing on the rocks or temporary scaffolding, over rapids and shoals, and spearing the fish as they appeared near the surface to leap the falls, or floundered in the rocks. On the lower Columbia, the fish were drawn ashore by rude seines. At Chinook point (opposite Astoria), the shore is a shelving bank of sand, three or four miles long, on which the fishermen were wont to haul the seines. The Anglo-Saxons soon availed themselves of this fine fishing grounds. The fish taken at this point were called "Chinook Salmon," in contradistinction to those taken at the falls and stood better in market. There not being many places along the banks of the river sufficiently sloping for the dragging of seines, another net was brought into requisition called the gill net. The meshes of this net are of such size as to admit the head of the fish sufficiently to entangle and hold it fast by the gills. The nets are about two fathoms wide with sinkers on one edge and small buoys on the other, which cause them to float perpendicularly when stretched in the stream. They vary in length from one hundred to three hundred fathoms. Two men with a boat attend each net. The net is extended across the channel and allowed to float down with the tide while the boat passes back and forth along the line of buoys, watching for fish and keeping the net aright.

The fish, ascending the river, thrusts its head through the meshes of the descending net and becoming entangled, disturb the buoys over it which immediately summons the men in the boat, who coming to the spot, lift that portion of the net, strike the fish a blow on the head, cast it into their boat and drop again the net. Thus they work till the boat is full of fish or they have drifted the proper distance when they take the net into the boat and go back to the fishery. Two men will sometimes catch three hundred fish in one night. "Drifting" is generally done at night so the fish cannot see the nets, but many were caught last season during the day in cloudy weather.

Packing at first was done by the fishermen who would make their nets, boats and barrels through the Autumn and Winter and fish during the run of Salmon, salting them in large tanks till the rush was over when they would transfer their catch to barrels. With the preservation of the fish in hermetically sealed cans began a great improvement in the business. The canneries also prepare outside of the fish season, for packing, but their consumption of fish is so great and rapid that they purchase fresh fish largely in addition to what their own men take, paying from twenty-five to thirty cents per fish. This furnishes an opportunity for fishermen (strictly speaking) to ply their avocation. A boat and net, bought for three hundred dollars, or rented on shares, is all the outfit needed.

When the first canning establishment began operating on the river, the manner of preserving the fish was said to be a secret of great depth, and marvelous stories were circulated to the effect that the man who possessed the mysterious knowledge, plied his art within the closed brick walls of a boiling room, so full of heat and steam that few could live within. By some means, however, others became familiar with the mystery, or supposed they were, and another cannery started, but something was lacking, the charm did not work, fish spoiled and several thousand dollars were lost. But in time others succeeded and now there seems to be but little secrecy about it, no more than in canning peaches or tomatoes. The fish are cut into pieces corresponding to the size of the can, and packed in raw, with a little brine, when the can is partly sealed and placed into a cauldron of boiling water till the fish is cooked.

The business, particularly the canning, has increased in profit and in magnitude the past year, and next season there will be double the facilities for preserving fish judging from present preparations. Eight canning establishments were in operation this last season. Now six more are being erected and additions made to the old ones. Last season but one steam tender was owned by the fisheries, next year there will be three, two small steam boats having been recently purchased for that purpose. These boats will be used to bring the fish from the different "drifts" to the cannery and in transporting their own freight generally. Cases of canned salmon ready for market are estimated to cost five dollars each, while they sell at home for seven to eight dollars, and are now quoted in the Australian market at sixteen dollars per case. Three of the fisheries this season put up about fifteen thousand cases each, clearing doubtless thirty thousand dollars apiece. The outlay for fixtures is chiefly for boats, nets and machinery for manufacturing the cans. Aside from what wharfing may be necessary, the buildings are cheap. A location is generally chosen where the channel approaches near the shore so as to render much wharfing unnecessary. The principal article of import used is tin which is brought in [?] and manufactured into cans at the fishery. The cases are bought ready made of our Oregon box manufactories by all the fisheries we believe, except Westport. In connection with that one is a saw mill which furnishes the lumber and makes its own boxes and barrels. The heads and trimmings of the fish were thrown away by all till the last season, when J. West of Westport utilized the heads by extracting the oil from them which proved to be a profitable experiment. It is to be hoped that more will do likewise hereafter.

Labor is generally performed by white men, though troubles incident to that kind of labor have caused one or two establishments to employ chinamen to do the indoor work. The fisheries are in isolated places where new hands cannot be secured in a moment. During the fishing season not a moment should be lost, as the fish should be preserved on the same day they are brought in. Losses have occurred by the laborers getting liquor and disqualifying themselves for labor for several days and suspending the work. Isolated locations are chosen with an eye to being removed from temptation. All the principal fisheries on the lower Columbia are within forty miles of Astoria.

An Inspector of Salmon was formerly appointed by the State, but as he could not visit the different fisheries when needed, he was obliged to trust much to the honesty of the packers, and the office was soon abolished. Now each firm puts its individual brand upon the packages sent out and stands or falls by its reputation.

A few fish are caught in traps formed of stakes driven in the bottom near shore. The principal danger encountered with the drift nets is the Seal which pursues and preys upon the Salmon. They get into the nets sometimes and being strong do more or less damage, though when captured compensate somewhat in oil for the harm done.

It might be well to mention another species of fish called the fall Salmon which enter the small creeks near the ocean in October and are much better for being dried and smoked than the spring Salmon as they have less fat. Large quantities are taken from the creek, at the Seaside House, just as they enter from the ocean. Several persons are there now engaged in salting and smoking them. With a small seine, two men drag out one and two hundred fine fish at each haul.

May 7, 1874 WA
WA Newspaper

THE SALMON FISHERIES.
Upper Astoria, Oregon

Large parties of visitors, from this city, have been to the upper-town cannery during the past week, and all express themselves well paid for the time spent in observing the workings of this new productive establishment, which is now in full operation. Over five hundred fish were brought in last Monday morning by the fishing fleet, and the operatives were in their busiest mood all that day. The process was watched that day by numerous visitors with interest, from the beginning, where the fish is first cleaned and washed, until it passes through the many hands and different processes and is finally put into the cans for shipment.

Construction on the upper-town cannery was commenced on last Christmas day. The firm is known as Badollet & Co., and is composed of five of the active business men of Astoria, viz: John Hobson, Geo. W. Warren, J. Badollet, H.S. Aiken and C. Leinenweber. Mr. Leinenweber is manager of the business affairs of the company. Mr. S.T. McKean is Secretary, J.T. Davis Superintendent of the baths, and W. Davis jr. Superintendent of the shops. The buildings are constructed over the bay with the exception of the main boarding house, and covers a space 70 by 280 feet, divided as follows: Store 20 by 40; main shop 40 by 120 two stories; tin shop 40 by 100; bath house 36 by 47, with seven large circular kettles; coal house 12 by 24, etc. The boarding-house is 20 by 40 two stories high. The buildings, together with machinery, stock on hand, and 400 tons of tin en route, cost $100,000. Sixty-two men are employed besides ten boats fishing, with 20 men. The Company expect to put up 20,000 cases of canned Salmon for export this year, the proceeds of which will amount to the snug little sum of from $140,000 to $160,000, all the expense of making which entails the disbursement of a handsome sum of money every month. The first shipment of a 1,000 cases goes out by the steamer this week. For water, and general convenience, the premises are very well situated, equal to the best on the river. With the receipt of Salmon in greater quantities the company are prepared to more than double their present working force.

BROOKFIELD, W.T.

This is the first Cannery above Astoria, located in a delightful spot on the territory side of the river, near the point known as Jim Crow. The proprietors are Joseph and A.J. Megler, Thomas S. Jewett, and J.S. Chambers, all of Astoria. Like the works at the upper-town, the Brookfield cannery was all built last Winter, and the present is the first season, for packing. The brand bears the firm name of Megler & Jewett.

Considering the time in which Megler & Jewett have been at work, (not to exceed six months), they have done something remarkable. The dock is 50 by 150 feet in size, with a T 34 by 150 feet, all covered in, and suitable for the largest sized vessels to lie along side. The buildings, machinery and stock, at the present time, amount to more than $60,000. The main shop is 40 by 160 feet in size, Wash-house, Bath-house, and Coal-house, 14 by 50; Mess-house, two stories, 24 by 40; Store 25 by 50, and numerous smaller buildings, comprise the working portion of the premises. The bath room is supplied with nine large square kettles, with a capacity for boiling 5,000 cans of fish at one bath. With the force of hands at present employed 10,000 cans can be manufactured daily, and the firm are prepared to put up, this season, 20,000 cases of four dozen one pound cans for export. They have 16 boats fishing, each carrying two men, besides 70 hands employed about the cannery in various capacities.

The location of the Brookfield works could not be improved. The site is a handsome one, commanding a view of the bay and river for miles up and down and the work already done on the grounds, shows it to be susceptible of a high state of cultivation. The residence grounds of Joseph and A.J. Megler, adjacent to the works, are handsomely laid off and appear very attractive.

Brookfield has only been a post office a few weeks, yet THE ASTORIAN reaches 24 bona fide subscribers at that place, all new this week with the exception of four, showing that it is a reading community. When the season for putting up Salmon closes, we understand that Megler & Jewett propose putting up green peas, fruit, etc., and to try the experiment of condensing milk for export. Here will be a fine opening for the agriculturist to dispose of his surplus products, and for some enterprising man to turn his attention to the production of milk for condensing.

May 14, 1874

A VISIT TO THE FISHERIES.

Last Thursday we gave a brief account of two canneries on the Columbia river, Astoria and Brookfield, since which time by invitation of Mr. Vin Cook, of the Clifton works, we have spent two days on the river, calling at every one of the canneries, except the Rainier establishment of R.D. Hume; and at some five of the packing establishments, where fish are put up in barrels, when there is a plentiful run and the canneries are stocked with Salmon.

THE CLIFTON CANNERY

Is a new establishment, constructed during the past winter by the Oregon Packing Company, E.E. Morgan's Sons, Agents, James W. and Vin. Cook proprietors. Before "a lick was struck" in the commencement of the Clifton cannery last fall, the site of that now busy place was only marked by a land slide which must have occurred at least half a century ago, forming a level plateau at the base of a precipitous mountain, giving the energetic proprietors an opportunity to branch out and cause the spot not only to blossom as the rose, but become a stirring factory for the employment of capital and numerous men in lucrative business. Clifton can boast of a cannery second to none on the river, in point of convenience, and the general details of water supply, fuel, and the facilities for shipping. The main buildings are commenced upon the wharf along the ship channel. The wharf is 150 feet front, by 100 feet depth; the tin shops are in the second stories of the filling and packing houses, each 50 by 100 feet in size with a covered arcade 100 feet square between, for salting, storing, etc., while the bath room, containing 18 kettles and three double furnaces, extends across the entire rear from the filling room, where the cans are prepared for the boilers to the packing room, where they receive the varnish and labels and go into the cases and out to the steamer or vessel for shipment. Twelve thousand five hundred pounds of fish can be placed into bath (boiling) at one time at this establishment, and the company are prepared to put up to 30,000 cases, of four dozen pound cans, the present season. They have a capital of not less than $100,000 invested in the business at Clifton, in buildings, machinery and stock, and at present give employment to 70 men on the premises, besides 34 fishermen.

THE CATCHING PROCESS.

About five o'clock a.m. Friday, after having spent a good agreeable time with Vin and his cheerful family, the day and evening previous, as we were about bidding Clifton good bye, and stood together on the dock waiting for Captain West's steamer *Carrie*, which was to convey us to Falkinburg's, the fisherman's central depot for the Woody Island "drift," we remarked to our friend that the canning process, if minutely described would be an entertaining item for perusal, and queried: "What is the first thing to be done," "The first item is to get the fish!" and with that remark we stepped on board the little steamer *Carrie* and were away for new scenes, Capt. John West of Westport, and Robert Watson of Manhattan, were on board, and like Mr. Cook, each were on a mission to solve the problem intimated by the reply to our question of the first thing to be done. Here were three candidates—for fish; and to them it was a matter of more moment than the affair of any three candidates for Congress, Governor, or Secretary of State, canvassing for votes. The question of Salmon was the one then under consideration, and the number of the catch was to decide the value thereof, and the prospects of the trade. Arriving at Falkinburg's we met the fleet of fishing craft, and soon transferred the contents to the steamer. Captain West was elected that morning by a plurality—of fish; but the aggregate count was less by considerable, than for the same period last year. It is a fact that the number and capacity of the canneries has this season doubled over that of 1873, and perhaps there is this year three nets in the river to one last year.—but it is nevertheless a fact that with all the extra preparations to receive and entertain the elegant fish, Messrs Salmon fail to appreciate such effort and do not come to time. The books of John West & Co. show that for the first twenty-five days of the last year, with but 10 boats fishing, his daily average was 412 Salmon. For a corresponding period this season with 21 boats (more than doubled), the daily average has been 355 Salmon. Any person conversant with figures can see from this showing what the condition of the market is likely to become. We will only venture one opinion, at present; that is that the river is now supplied with all the canning establishments that the run will warrant, and that those who have discouraged parties from contracting for round lots on the expectation that fish would be cheaper, in consequence of the increased preparations for putting them up, will find themselves mistaken. There are thirteen canneries now on the river, with an average capital of $65,000 each—an aggregate of not less than $845,000—to say nothing of boats and nets, employed in the fishing business this year, within 67 miles of Astoria, calling for from 2,000 to 2,500 men, and yet, up to this date none but the fishermen are busy to exceed half time. These are the facts, and they speak for legislation to protect the Salmon, which we have hitherto advocated, and will in due time refer to again.

A FISHING OUTFIT

Consists of a good net from 125 to 175 fathoms in length, and 14 to 20 feet in depth, buoyed and leaded for drifting, with meshes of 8 to 8 1/4 inches; 2d, a good boat, 24 feet long, sharp at both ends, with two sets of oars and a sail; 3d, coffee pot and grub pail; 4th, water proof clothing. With this outfit two men start fishing, usually about five o'clock p.m., and continue for 12 to 15 hours. There is constant exposure, and no small risk, in this part of the business, but the fisherman throws his net into the stream hopefully, watches it patiently, and works with it energetically, whenever a fish becomes entangled in the meshes, or an ugly snag, or seal, sturgeon, or sea-lion interferes with the ordinary course. There is no time to idle away in a fishing boat; and the drift of a fisherman's life is not altogether lovely. Five steamers are employed exclusively by canneries, picking up fish and jobbing from place to place. The *Otter*, Capt. Fisher, is under charter to G.W. and Wm. Hume, the *Carrie* is for John West & Co., Watson Bros & Co., and J.W. and V. Cook, the *Jane West* is for Joseph Hume, the *Oneatta* for R.D. Hume, and the *St. Patrick* for Hapgood & Company. After the fish are brought in and counted, the net is to be looked after, then the little boat crews take refreshments and sleep till evening again, leaving the canneries in full operation;

WORKING UP THE FISH

Is the most interesting portion—next to receiving the coin, perhaps it is the pleasantest part of the work to proprietors. To one side of the establishment there is a receptacle where the fish are taken. The first man to "lay hold of" a Salmon there is the dresser—and he lays on hands with a vengeance, trimming fins, heads, entrails and tails, as he goes along at the rate of 1,000 to 1,500 fish daily, which passes thro' a series of tubs at each of which the fish is washed, scraped and scrubbed, until it reaches the cutter. One turn of the knife cuts the Salmon into four inch pieces, and the next grade brings it to a junction with the cans on a straight line for the bathrooms. Filling, topping, soldering done, into the bath with 3,200 other cans goes the one we had our eye on. After a time out they come, the air vent is opened, the can again sealed, into a hotter bath it goes for another spell, then out again and into the lye bath, then the shower bath, next to the packing room, and away to its destination. Were fish plentiful, a set of hands would be employed to each separate department, but as it is now one set can more than keep ahead of the supply of fish at each cannery. The following establishments were visited by us on Friday last:

Astoria, Oregon	Badollet & Co
Brookfield, W.T	Megler & Jewett
Glen Ella, W.T	J. L. Hepburn
Bay View, W.T	R. D. Hume
Clifton, W.T	W. & V. Cook
Manhattan, Oregon	Watson Bros & Co.
Cathlamet, W.T	Warren & Co.
Westport, Oregon	John West & Co.
Waterford, W.T	Hapgood & Co.
Eureka, W.T	Joseph Hume
Eagle Cliff, W.T	Geo. W. Hume
" "	William Hume

R.D. Hume has an establishment at Rainier in connection with the one at Bay View, making thirteen canneries on the river. The process of canning fish is very much the same at each one. At some of the places visited we had but a few moments to spare in making observations, and only for the kindness of Capt. Fisher, of the steamer *Otter*, who picked us up at Clifton, on the return from Falkinburg's and stopped for us at various points, making special landings, and in various ways accommodating us (all of which is duly appreciated). We should not have been able to get around, even hurriedly, in one day. We found the managers and employes at each and every point, so far as we were able to observe, obliging gentlemen who seemed willing to make us acquainted with all the facts of the business, and without wishing to trespass upon their valuable time, or make impertinent inquiries respecting minutia, we may have been somewhat reserved, and still our wishes were anticipated, and we returned at night with a fund of information on the subject not otherwise readily acquired. Jointly, if the fish can be obtained, the Columbia river canneries could this year put up, (as they have the preparations for doing so), 300,000 cases, containing 14,400,000 cans, of one pound each, valued at $2,100,000. To produce which they pay $1,000,000 for tin and manufacturing cans, boxes, etc., and distribute $525,000 among the fishermen for fish, $26,000 for incidental expenses, leaving a balance of $18,231 to each, net profits for the season. We say this might be done could they get the fish, but just will be—none can tell.

THE MARKET FOR FISH

Has hitherto been confined to foreign trade, so far as the Columbia river is concerned, but the business at present discloses the fact that America furnishes a market for much more than the supply. St. Louis, Chicago, Memphis and New Orleans are already here with orders in advance of the fish, and from what we have seen there is every reason to predict that the city of New York would call upon the Columbia river for every case before another season, so that our canneries may be certain of realizing by increased prices, a portion at least of any losses they may sustain by reason of a short supply.

THE MATTER OF MEN.

At nearly every cannery on the Columbia river, the chief reliance for help seems to be based upon the Chinese, and the fellows appear to ply their several vocations skillfully, with limited instruction. Mr. Wm. Hume employs no celestials [Chinese] in any capacity, and appears to be qualified with a proper understanding of human nature to judge of the merits of a man on short trial, a rare qualification, it must be admitted, and as a consequence he has an energetic set of men about him. The matter of labor has been one of serious consideration in this business. The season is a short one, a great many men have to be employed, and in no other branch of the industries is greater system required, it must be clockwork—on, on, from the start, no going back, and to utilize the boats by making every minute count for sixty seconds, is the aim in everything about a cannery. There is no room for any drones at a Columbia river cannery—and the men generally take as much pride in that fact as the employers. In war times what a regiment could be raised from out of these men. Many of them have seen service of that character, and from the fishing fleet could be picked many a hero who would be a credit to the navy. Success attend them all—individually and collectively, is our wish. To the many whom we met on that day, so imperfectly described in this brief account of the visit—to whom we feel under obligation for favors extended, we return our thanks.

N.S. Welch came near drifting out to sea one night recently, while fishing in a fog for Salmon. He saved his net, boat, etc., and came up on the Varuna the next day.

Apr. 30, 1874 WA

The body of Charles Westborg, who fell overboard several weeks ago one night, when passing to the steam tug *Brenham*, was found last Sunday.

Seven men have fallen into the river at Astoria within one week. Fortunately but one of this batch was drowned.

Feb. 26, 1876 WA

S.W. Childs, who was reported lost last night, says "it is a mistake, and that he is good for lots of salmon yet." During the severe blow yesterday morning from three to five o'clock, the welfare of fishermen at work in the bay was one of anxiety. One boat is known to have been lost—as it passed Chinook, the cries of the fishermen in it were to no purpose, as no boat could be launched, in the condition of the surf, as it was then, to go to the assistance of those in distress, and an empty boat, badly demolished on the beach below Chinook probably tells of disaster and loss of life. Mr. Childs' boat and others were reported missing last evening. The hope is that all may turn up safe. Mr. C. did not go out Sunday night. Others supposed to be lost, may have remained at home also.

May 16, 1876 DA

We regret to hear that our friend S.W. Childs lost his boat Monday night, during the gale, on Sand Island. But in all disasters there are some grains for comfort. In this case, Mr. Childs and his boat-puller saved themselves. We hope to hear that the boat may not become a total loss.

May 30, 1876 DA

A private letter from Badollet & Co's factory, dated June 7th says: We have reason to believe that Ed. Williams and Johnson, boat puller, two of our fishermen have been lost, not having been seen or heard of since Sunday evening, of which you will please make note in your paper.

June 10, 1876 WA

Hope and search has been abandoned, for Williams and Johnson, fishermen for Badollet & Co., who were lost a week ago last night. We understand that the boat came ashore north of Cape Hancock about eight miles, and the net was found south of Point Adams about six miles, just how true the statement is we are unable to say. Williams was a daring spirit, excitable, and it is presumed ventured so near to the bar that return was impossible. He formerly boarded at Mrs. Daggetts. Johnson was formerly a deck hand on the *Beaver*. We do not know that either have any kinsfolk in this country.

June 17, 1876 WA

Sophie Daggett's boarding house was on the northeast corner of 11th and Franklin in Astoria where the Arlington Hotel was located later.

Mr. C. Leinenweber returned last night from his search after Williams and Johnson, the lost fishermen. He found the sail, two oars and eighteen fathom of the net down the beach, fourteen miles south of the bar, but the men were no where to be seen, dead nor alive.

June 18, 1876 WA

Charley Brown, employed by the Anglo American Packing company, was the fisherman who went out to sea in company with the boat picked up by the *Forward*. He crossed the bar on the morning of Monday, May 28th, and finding himself fixed for a voyage, secured everything on board his boat, and prepared to make the best of it. He set sail for Shoalwater bay, which he reached in safety, then continued on up to the portage of Bear river, reaching there on Tuesday when he hired a farmer to pull his boat across the portage with cattle. On Wednesday he launched his boat into the Columbia again, and began fishing. He met with very good success, and was the first man to hitch on to the tow line of the tug Thursday morning with 31 fine Salmon in his boat. He was joyfully welcomed home by all, having been out three nights, and given up as lost.

June 9, 1877 WA

An Italian, name unknown, fishing for John A. Devlin & Co., went to sea Sunday night, May 27th, and had a very stormy time of it. He came in alive but his companion died soon after getting to sea, the first night. He struck the beach in Tillamook county, just north of the Necarney, on Monday last and by the aid of Temple and Z.N. Seeley and Jacob R. Cromwell pulled his boat upon the beach, and he is now on his way to Astoria and is expected to arrive here to-day. The poor fellow has had a very hard time. His life was spared, by the accident of having caught a sturgeon. For several days he clung to the bottom of his boat at sea turning it on the 8th day, before he reached shore. Mr. Seeley arrived here yesterday.

June 9, 1877 WA

Mr. Thomas Logan is the man who landed one of Badollet and Co's boats below the Seaside after being outside three days and three nights [on the ocean]. Mr. Logan's presence of mind enabled him to save his net, boat and catch (amounting to 56 salmon). The boat arrived safely at the cannery. On

Wednesday a portion of the expenses of his eventful trip was defrayed by a portion of the catch he had in his boat when he came ashore. Mr. Logan is the husband of Minnie Myrtle Miller and the dangerous voyage he made terminating so happily as it did may be the means of inspiring the muses enabling Mrs. Logan to produce something elegant on the subject.

June 15, 1877 DA

On Saturday night the fishermen employed in Kinney's boat *No. 19*, on taking up their net near the spar buoy off Smith's Point, found the body of a dead man entangled therein. They brought the body to town and notified acting coroner Fox of the circumstance. The body was conveyed to the engine house [fire station] and a jury summoned and an inquest held. The result of the coroner's inquest proved the body to be that of August March, a Prussian about 38 years of age, who was accidently drowned by falling, while asleep, from a fishing boat on the evening of the eighth of June.

June 23, 1877 WA

LINES.

Written for THE ASTORIAN

It seems in the dim, dim yore,
Yet it is not long ago,
Since an aged fisher drew ashore
His boat on the sands of snow.

His locks were white, and rolled
From his brow like the edge of the sea.
His hands were feeble and cold,
And dreamy and silent was he.

When he pushed his boat from the sands,
To fish in the sullen deep,
I laughed and clapped my hands,
And sung myself to sleep.

Wherever the subtle moon
Beckoned the murky tide,
Through the deep nights inky noon,
Where the golden salmon glide.

In a world apart from our own,
For the shiny ones are cold;
Without voice or whisper or moan,
And armored in scales of gold.

He drifted in perilous ways,
And his child the rapt night long,
Lay dreaming of crowns and bays
In a world of light and song.

Now the gray tides blow and blow,
Like shadows along the lea;
And the sea tide rivulets flow
On to their homes in the sea.

By the solemn moon enticed,
The tides are murmuring yet,
But he was called of Christ,
And he left his boat and net.

MINNIE MYRTLE LOGAN,
July 28, 1877 WA

THE LONE GRAVE ON THE BEACH.

The tempest is wild to night,
And high breaks the wave
When the moon sheds its light
On a desolate grave—
Just above the water's reach—
The lone grave on the beach.

Its secret, all its own,
Lo! these many long years—
No cold, gray stone,
No sorrowing mourner's tears,
To tell by eye or by word to teach,
Who lies in the lone grave on the beach.

And e'en yet the waves may break
And on the cold rocks resound
In vain tempts the secret to wake,
As the fleeting years roll round
Till the last day's summons shall reach
The sad, lone grave on the beach.

LAWRENCE ELLMORE.
Clatsop, Aug. 24, 1877.
Printed in Oct. 13, 1877 DA

Death of Col. H.K. Stevens and Frank Fowles

Last Thursday evening between five and six o'clock, a fishing boat left Astoria for Chinook, carrying six persons.

Messrs. Fred. Woodham of this city, Henry Pierce, William Devins, Jos. Bertrand, Col. H.K. Stevens and Frank Fowles. They had proceeded about half way across the bay when the weather began to be pretty rough, and the sail slipped out of the hands of Fowles, who was steering the boat, and in getting the sail back again, through bad steering, the boat capsized. A woman saw the boat upset from the territory shore and gave the alarm, when Eben Pietit manned a boat and immediately started for the rescue of the party, but the wind was then blowing a gale and the tide was against them, so that it was nearly three hours before the unfortunate men were reached. Fowles drowned in a few minutes after the boat upset, and Mr. Stevens hung on for about an hour, then he was drowned. This left Messrs. Pierce, Woodham, Devins and Bertrand clinging to the boat still bottom up, and in an almost exhausted condition when they were picked up and taken to Chinook. It seems a miracle that any of them were saved as the weather was very chilly, and they were in the water a long time, dashing by the fury of a rough sea against the boat almost every instant of the time. Mr. Woodham returned to Astoria on Sunday. From a letter received from Mr. Bertrand we gain the principal points of their rescue. Mr. Bertrand says that Fowles was intoxicated and would not let one of the sober men of the party touch the helm. We believe Mr. Fowles was a single man, Mr. Stevens leaves a wife and two children in this city. He was a pioneer of Chinook, but for several years past, up to very recently, has resided in Oysterville.

August 28, 1877

Mr John Corcoran, at one time on the police force of Astoria, and previously employed in the same capacity in Portland, lost his life by drowning in this city about two o'clock yesterday. The particulars, as near as we were able to ascertain, are that that he, with four others who had come to the city from upper Astoria to attend the workingmens jubilee and torch-light procession, continuing to "ratify" after the multitude had dispersed and became a little over-joyful, and in attempting to embark in a small boat for home, the boat upset at the landing near the corner of Water and West-sixth street, where all were thrown into the water, and Corcoran lost his life. John was his own worst enemy. With the exception of his dissipating habits he was in every way a very worthy and estimable young man.

John Corcoran's body was found and decently interred, yesterday.

December 15, 1877 WA

March 23, 1878 WA

COLUMBIA RIVER SALMON FISHERY
By Mrs. Nelly E. Megler, Brookfield, Washington Terr.

The salmon canning establishments on the Columbia river are situated both on the Oregon and Washington territory sides, the nearest being about fifteen and the farthest sixty miles from its mouth. During the fall and winter months at these establishments, the cans and nets are made and everything got in readiness for the busy season. About the first of April the salmon begin to come into the river, but not in great numbers till the middle of that month, and sometimes not before the first of May; from that time till the first of August the canneries are in operation. For fishing, gill nets are most generally used; these are made large, the usual size being 250 fathoms long, 20 feet deep, with an 8

23

3/8 inch mesh; the boats used are also very large and are nicely fitted up. Two men occupy each boat, one to tend the net and the other to row; the fishermen employed are always white men (so distinguished from Chinamen), many of them being Sweeds and Fins [sic]. The canneries own most of the boats and nets, which they lease to the net tender, and he hires his rower. The price paid for fish varies with the season; last year 50 cents per fish was paid. The salmon in this river are probably the largest in the world; they average from 20 to 24 pounds each, and I saw one that weighed 84 pounds, but, of course, that was something unusual.

There is generally a freshet in the river for about two weeks, during the month of June, when the fishing is done during the day, but at other times all fishing is done in the night, for the salmon are very shy and the water at other times so clear, that even by tanning the net, they detect it.

It is a pretty sight, in the early twilight of a pleasant day, to see the boats, with sails all spread, skimming along the water, on their way to the fishing grounds. Then it seems as though the fisherman's life must be a pleasant one, but when, as is more often the case, it rains—as it can only rain in Oregon—and with the nights intensely dark, the romance vanishes; and as we draw the curtain to shut out the dreariness, it is with an earnest hope that no boat will be capsized by the gale, or that in the darkness and fog, none may drift outside the bar, for the river is rapid and broad. Probably at no point where fishing is done is it less than three miles wide and in some places six or seven.

Each cannery has a steamboat which is sent out in the morning to tow the fishing boats home. These steamers will tow sometimes thirty boats at one time. By this means the boats are usually in by 9 o'clock in the morning, giving the fishermen the day for sleep, so they are able to go fishing the next night again. When the boats come in, the nets are all given to a net-tender, who examines them, mends all rents, and gets them ready for the men at night.

The fish, as they are landed on the wharf, are counted; then a Chinaman takes them, and, by quick strokes with a knife, the heads, tails and fins are dis-severed; then he splits, cleans and throws them into a large tank of salt water. Another Chinaman takes the scales, slimes and thoroughly washes them; then they are taken to a machine that cuts them in pieces to fit the cans; these are taken to the fillers, who press them in cans and salt them, each can receiving the same amount; then the tops are put in. The machine that cuts these tops punches a hole in each. Now the solderers receive the cans and solder the tops on, and also the hole in the tops. These cans are, or supposed to be air tight; they are passed through the testing tank, and if no leak is discernable they are ready for cooking. This is done in most canneries with steam. In this way they are cooked one hour; then they are taken out, a hole is punctured in them to let out the air, and immediately re-soldered. After this process, they are ready for the last cooking; this is done in steam-tight tanks. When taken from these tanks they are dipped in strong lye to take off all grease. After cooling they are again tested and the perfect ones lacquered. When this is dry they are labeled, and when thoroughly dry are cased and ready for shipping. Most of

24

this work is done by Chinamen, who work well, if they have a good overseer, and are very expeditious.

Before closing this article I will give a little description of the places where these establishments are situated. The canneries are invariably built over the water on piles. Back of these, on the banks of the river are clustered a few dwellings, with generally a pretty cottage, where the proprietor or foreman resides. Back of these are high bluffs, covered with evergreen trees, mostly spruce, hemlock and fir. These might rival the big trees of California, if not in diameter, in height. The mail is brought to these places daily by the boats plying between Portland and Astoria. Of course this description does not apply to the canneries situated at Astoria.

Just now I hear that Mr. E.C. Rufus, who runs Badollet & Co's boat *No. 10*, was capsized this morning. Himself and boat puller were in the water two hours before being rescued. The boat righted and net saved. It seems that the fishermen are venturing too near the bar for their own safety.

April 19, 1878

About 1 o'clock P.M., at high tide yesterday, one of Badollet & Co's fishing boats capsized near Scarborough hill, the fishermen clung to the bottom and were rescued by one of Watson's fishing boats. The net and boat are probably lost, as the wind was blowing a gale at the time.

April 20, 1878

One of Jos. Hume's fishing boats was seen returning to the cannery at Knappton about noon yesterday with only one man and part of a net. Whether the other man was lost or not we did not learn. The wind was blowing severely.

April 20, 1878 WA

Messrs. Badollet & Co's fishing boat *No. 12* in charge of Nicholas Devinich, capsized last night below Scarborough hill. The occupants of the boat saved themselves with difficulty. The net was picked up by Mr. John Lewis, who runs Watson Bros. boat *No. 17*, who had the meanness to demand the sum of $100 for a few minutes work, refusing to give up the net unless paid that sum. Messrs. B. & Co. tendered him $20, which he finally concluded to accept rather than to go to law. The boat was picked up by Mr. Peter Rosset, who had the manliness to charge nothing for the same.

April 20, 1878 WA

About 3 o'clock yesterday morning, a fishing boat was upset while under sail in the river near the city, the wind being very strong. The boat was picked up by two fishing boats passing about two hours afterwards, with two men setting on the bottom, and brought to the shore. The boat belonged to Wm. Hume, of Eagle Cliff, and upon righting her it was found that the night's catch, which consisted of thirteen fish, and a few utensils had been lost.

April 20, 1878 WA

Four fishing boats are reported in a bad condition on Chinook beach, having been driven ashore in a gale night before last. The boats are badly damaged and unable to leave the beach without assistance. The nets are mostly saved, one or two were buried in the sand so deep that it required some labor to raise them.

April 27, 1878 WA

A fishing boat belonging to A. Booth & co. was capsized opposite the city on Sunday. The steamer *Quickstep* was lying at the wharf and was immediately dispatched to the rescue. The fishermen and net were taken on board the steamer and the boat towed to the dock, where it was righted and the men started on the way home rejoicing.

May 4, 1878 WA

Messrs. Devlin & Co. received a private letter last evening from Mr. P.J. McGowan, of Chinook, that a boat marked *D. & Co., No. 7*, had come ashore on the beach with the net. One of the men was found entangled in the net, lifeless, while the other is supposed to be drowned.

May 5, 1878 WA

Night before last and yesterday morning, the weather was quite rough for fishing in this vicinity. The *Quickstep* noticed a blue boat piled up on Chinook spit yesterday morning so high as to be beyond reach. Capt. Cousins says he could not see any men in nor about her, but that they ought to have been there safely, as the boat was right side up.

May 18, 1878 WA

Drowned on the Bar

Mr. Martin Grain, a Swede, comparatively a stranger here, but employed by the Astoria fishery as a fisherman, lost his life on Wednesday night by a foolhardy attempt to fish on the bar, only accidentally drifting to that locality of real danger in a small fishing boat. It appears that he threw out his net on the south side of Sand island, and, drifting down past the island was caught by the breakers and the boat, which was one of the largest and best ones of the large Kinney cannery, was completely turned over end-wise, throwing both men, and every movable thing into the sea. The cries of the men were distinctly heard, and one of J.G. Megler & Co's boats near by went to their relief, saving the boat-puller, the net and the boat, but poor Martin Grain was lost. We are unable to say whether deceased leaves a family or any friends in this country.

July 6, 1878 WA

We are in receipt of a pass-book and a letter from P.J. McGowan of Chinook, yesterday. Mr. McGowan says: "Yesterday, July 11th, about 12 o'clock, two men in a blue boat, *No. 18*, (so the persons present say), left a drowned man in front of my place, giving no information respecting him. He was brought on shore, and after we were through fishing, we buried him. On his person was found a small silver watch, silver chain attached, common smoking pipe and tobacco, a little tin salve-box, a small pocket-knife, two pieces of pencil, and what appears to be a pass-book, which I send you for identification. The man bears evident signs of being foully dealt with.

P.J. McGOWAN

July 20, 1878 WA

Herbert, a bright young child of Capt. J.H.D. Gray, met with a sad accident yesterday afternoon while playing about the dock. He was last seen about 3 o'clock, and not again until about 5 o'clock when he was noticed by some children floating in the river below the Astoria fishery, when all life had gone. How it happened no one seemed to know. He would be four years old on the 28th inst.

Oct. 19, 1878 WA

A fishing boat from the Fishermen's Packing company, capsized about one mile off their cannery during a severe squall yesterday. A boat was launched from Booth & Co., and manned by G. Consolini, Joe Massa, Antoine Necrean and John Leika who very galantly pulled for the sunken boat and succeeded in rescuing both the men and boat.

Apr. 18, 1879 WA

We are informed that the citizens living near Ilwaco have found, and decently buried, the remains of a child, apparently two or three years of age between Ilwaco and the mouth of the Wallicut river. One of the arms was partly covered with a sleeve made of brown colored woolen goods, cut straight, trimmed with a black braid three sixteenths of an inch wide, passing twice around the cuff about one inch apart. Other portions of the body were found scattered along the beach. The remains were buried near Mr. Brown's place.

Apr. 18, 1879 WA

The body of a man was also picked up on the sea-beach, between the farms of Capt. Eastbrooks and L.A. Loomis. The head showed the effect of severe bruises. The feet were incased in short gum boots.

Apr. 18, 1879 WA

The remains of the man picked up on the weather beach have been identified as Martz, the Grays river mail carrier.

Apr. 18, 1879 WA

Capt. B.F. Stevens of Badollet and Co's steamer *Katata* informs us that night before last the swell was the roughest he has seen it for years near the bar. It was fearful in Bakers bay. The *Edith* lost her gang plank off the deck, and men were compelled to hold on to the life boat to keep it from going overboard. The plank was recovered.

The body of a man was picked up on the weather beach about five miles south of Oysterville road. The body was dressed in a blue sacque coat, with dark woolen pants, woolen check shirt, gum boots and oil skin coat. He had been a man apparently 175 to 180 pounds weight, about 5' 10" high. The body seemed to have been in the water a week to ten days.

A boat and net was towed into the cape yesterday morning. The bottom was filled with water and appeared to have gone out to sea and back again. The men are missing. It is a private boat, with only the license number on it, 494, issued to Eli Ipson, painted blue.

One of Bradley and Davis boats lost a net night before last, but found it in the edge of the breakers, too far gone for rescue. Net probably lost.

Fishermen should take into account the present high stage of water in the river which makes the slack and tides very different, in the vicinity of the bar.

May 30, 1879 DA

FISHING ON THE BAR.

Yesterday evening at sun set, the sea was calm at the bar on the Columbia, and up to the light-house. Several fishermen spread their seines along the water, between the point at the batteries and Sand island. Some time in the night a wind sprang up from the south, and the breakers set in towards the shore. Early this morning a blue fishing boat was discovered capsized, and at the rocks close to the light-house. Two boats and six men went round the point from the wharf, near the suttlers store, and brought in the boat and seine. These men reported that the two fishermen in the wrecked boat were drowned.

Soon after this it was discovered that a very long seine was in the breakers, and no boat near it. A steamer passed round to it, but it was afoul, and could not be recovered. So when the tide passes out towards noon to-day, it will take the seine into the ocean. The property belonged to two Italians who were drowned. The opinion seems to prevail amongst some of the fishermen on the bay that there are better fishing grounds west of Sand island, than higher up in the bay.

But I am assured by Captain Hewett that it is extremely dangerous to fish on these grounds. The sea may appear calm and all appearances fair, when all of a sudden a breeze may spring up, and the breakers begin to roll in towards shore, and a large wave may come in behind the boats and capsize them in a moment. In that case the men would be drowned, and the property perhaps lost. Fishermen should take warning of these facts. Breakers are rolling northward, along the west side of Sand island, at a fearful rate this morning. No marvel that the *Great Republic* broke up where she ran aground. Nothing is seen of the wreck now but the wheels and the walking beam.

Six o'clock P.M. Another seine lost to-day in the breakers, and the two passed out to sea. Part of one of them was seen this evening, a little west of McKinzie head, entangled among the rocks.

DAVID NEWSOME. *May 31, 1879 DA*

Another ship wreck occurred in this vicinity last Friday. Our late eastern correspondent, Dan J. Ingalls, swamped in Lewis and Clarke river with a cargo of hay and shingles on a schooner belonging to his neighbor Elijah Jeffers.

June 1, 1879 DA

Mr. Jas. W. Welch returned from the Weather beach north of Ilwaco yesterday, where he had been as N. G. of Beaver lodge of Odd Fellows, by direction of the lodge, searching for the body of Henry Lack, a member of Chemeketa lodge Salem. Mr. Welch informs us that five bodies have been washed up by the surf this year north of north-head. As a general thing the bodies are not properly buried, and he thinks that the people should club together, secure a site and be better prepared to bury the poor unfortunates whose bodies come in under such circumstances from the sea.

June 1, 1879 DA

Body Recovered.

Mr. Thomas B. Williams, light keeper at North cove, Shoalwater bay, writes to us that on the 25th the body of a man was picked up and buried about three miles from there. His features were not recognizable. He appeared to be about five feet nine inches in height. He was dressed in linen drawers, check pants, small dark blue coat, and wore gaiters with white cotton socks. There was found in his pockets two dollars and sixty cents in silver; three assorted sleeve buttons; gold thimble; silver plated fruit pocket knife, with A.D.B. engraved on; a double hair comb and steel cork screw. "I have the above described articles in my possession. I will be glad to send the articles found on the body to relatives or friends who may identify the person by the above description."

June 1, 1879 DA

The boat in which Mr. Henry Lack was fishing belongs to R.D. Hume & Co. and bears the license number of 269, his own boat is in the city. He leaves a sister in Michigan. His mother lives in England. As the body has not yet been recovered, any information will be thankfully received by Beaver Lodge No. 35, I.O.O.F.

June 1, 1879 DA

OUT OF THE JAWS OF DEATH.

Last Friday night Badollet & Co.'s No. 1 came up missing, and no trace of the men nor boat could be found until yesterday morning, when the net-tender, Mr. E.D. Marvin, and his boat-puller Lewis Larsen, arrived at the cannery. They had a very thrilling adventure. Mr. Marvin says he began taking up his net, as it didn't run to suit him in Bakers bay, and was wholly thrown off his guard by the rapidity of the current. In the net he found several large sturgeon and snags which interfered with the taking of it in, and the boat was swamped in the breakers. An accident happened that stopped his watch, which makes the hour at two minutes past 11 o'clock. They lost the oars, sail, anchor etc., but managed to hold on to the net, which Mr. Marvin believes was the sole measure of saving themselves. The net acted as ballast, and at the same time was so buoyant that it enabled them to keep themselves above water. After passing through the breakers, they picked up a piece of scantling, and by hard work got the boat bailed out, then improvised a sail, and started in, from a point about fifteen miles off shore, abreast of Shoalwater bay. They came through the surf opposite the Seaview house, and Messrs. Stout and Reed, and the family rendered them assistance, and the boat was hauled across to Ilwaco on Sunday. Mr. Marvin was warmly welcomed at the cannery. He says he has ran some desperate chances on the Frazer, upper Columbia and Colorado rivers, but this is the closest call of any. He had to cut the web out of his net finally to get a line before landing in the surf, and lost all of it in landing, but saved the boat. His steering oar was made of a piece of the flooring of the boat. He speaks in terms of highest praise of Mr. and Mrs. Stout, their daughter and Mr. Reed for kindness and attention.

June 6, 1879 WA

ANOTHER BODY FOUND.

The body of an unknown person was found on the weather beach, Pacific county, Washington Territory, near W.D. Tylor's residence May 27th, apparently a drowned fisherman, probable age 25 or 30, full six feet tall, stout built, full face, smooth shaved, except a thin brown mustache, dark thick hair, strong front teeth, no marks of violence on the body except a flesh wound in front of right ear, new light oil coat on, new gum boots, blue blouse, three shirts, dark pants, nothing found on the body except a pocket knife, waterproof match box and a light silk handkerchief, left side pants pocket torn off; probably been drowned three or four weeks. The remains after an examination were placed in a box, and decently buried above high water mark, under direction of Andrew Olsen, justice of the peace

June 6, 1879 WA

Another boat, unknown, capsized in the breakers yesterday abreast of Cape Hancock. Our informant could not tell whether the men were saved or not.

June 13, 1879 WA

The Italian taken from a boat which went to sea on the 3d, and returned on the 6th, more dead than alive is still in the hospital at Fort Stevens. He was in Wm. Hume's *No. 8* boat.

June 13, 1879 WA

Boat *No. 22*, from Cooks cannery, Clifton, attempted to save a man who was clinging to the bottom of a boat on the 5th, but were compelled to abandon the effort. It is not known who he was.

June 13, 1879 WA

Friday evening, about six o'clock boat *No. 569* belonging to the Astoria Packing company was struck by a sea below Sand island which completely ended the boat end over end. The net was lost but afterwards picked up by one of Watson Bros. boats. The men swam ashore on the island and were brought to the city.

June 13, 1879 WA

MAN DROWNED.

BAYVIEW, July 1, 1879

We regret to inform you of the loss by drowning this morning of one of our fishermen, named Charles Hendrickson. It occurred about 5 o'clock and just off Tongue point. The boat puller, who returned with the boat, states that they were under full sail, and Hendrickson was forward changing the sail some way, when he suddenly lost his footing and fell overboard. He noticed him rise above the water but once, for a moment and he disappeared entirely. The boat being under sail, it was impossible for him to stop it in time to render assistance. The body will probably go ashore on the Washington territory side. He is said to be a Russian Finn and unmarried and if he has any relatives in this country, we are not aware of it. Please mention this fact in the Astorian.

Yours very truly,
R.D. HUME
per F.M. Bartholow.

July 3, 1879 DA

THE 1880'S

Many exaggerated statements were afloat yesterday concerning the loss of boats, nets and men fishing, night before last. We could not get reliable data to base anything like a correct report upon. No doubt some persons lost their lives, but as to who they were, or to what cannery they belonged, etc., we are still unable to say.

The body which was brought to Astoria by the steamer *Quickstep* yesterday is supposed to be the remains of Mr. A.C. Slippen, whose loss was noted in THE ASTORIAN of the 23d ult., when he attempted to go from Astoria to Deep river in a small boat. He leaves a family in Washington territory. The body was found floating, standing erect in the water, the breast, shoulders and head just above the water, his hat still on. The remains were taken in charge by officers at the morgue, for christian burial.

May 5, 1880 DA

Monday night was a bitter night for the fishermen. Mr. Joseph Hume's steamer *Quickstep* arrived from Knappton yesterday at half past nine o'clock A.M., with her colors at half-mast, which drew a crowd of people together at the landing. Capt. Turner had the body of a man on board which he had picked up afloat in the bay, and two of Devlin and company's boats in tow, one of which was swamped. He reported one of the Astoria Fishing company's boats ashore at Chinook, and the net on the sands; and had information from Capt. Pease, of the *Edith*, that one of Booth and company's and one of Badollet and company's boats were lost.

May 5, 1880 DA

The most reliable reports concerning disasters to fishing boats night before last, comes from Capt. W.P. Whitcomb of the steamer *Gen. Canby*, who says that four boats came into Baker's bay without men or gear, yesterday morning. One other boat of the Aberdeen Packing company had not been heard from at noon; one of the same companys boats attempted to get into Wallicut, capsized, and one of the men was drowned. Four other boats were reported by reliable persons in the breakers, swamped, without men in them, half a mile below Scarboro hill. The men are possibly on shore, with their nets, and safe. At least it is hoped so.

May 5, 1880 DA

CASUALTIES.
Great Loss of Life and Property

Joseph Hume has picked up a large yellow boat. Kinney's *No. 6* is reported to have lost one man. Peter J. Blagan, an independent fisherman is reported lost. Two of J.G. Megler & Co.'s boats are supposed to be among the fleet lost. Wm. Hume's *No. 10*, Mr. Geo. Adams, a noble good man, is reported lost. There is no telling the amount of damages, nor loss of life by the storm of Tuesday night. All sorts of rumors are afloat. We give only such as we feel justified in placing any confidence in. The Anglo-American Packing company's *No. 11* drifted out to sea. Men and gear supposed to be lost. Two boats and nets were picked up yesterday morning afoul of the barkentine *North Bend*, lying at Grays dock. Many boats came in yesterday without a fish and the men in them were thankful that they had saved their lives. The steamers *Katata*, *Edith* and *Rip Van Winkle*, had a sorry time of it trying to lay at anchor near Sand Island. Mr. Kyle and partner report that they, with others, were two days on Sand Island, no food, fire nor other comforts. Hans Hansen of Geo. W. Hume's *No. 28* is reported lost; also Henry Heinson of boat *32*, same cannery. Jas. Hansen of *32* was saved. A few weather bound fishermen return grateful thanks for generous hospitalities extended to them by members of Hapgoods boats at Tongue point yesterday morning. Mr. Acklan reports seeing two men on the bottom of a blue boat, lead colored bottom, nearing the breakers yesterday morning. He could do nothing to save the men, and they bid him farewell by tipping their hats as they entered the jaws of death. It is said that one of the Eagle boats in charge of big Mike (name unknown to us) picked up the crews of two lost boats and put into a safe place above Tongue point. During the night a drift log struck Mike's boat, and the six men drowned.

May 7, 1880 WA

On Tuesday night last Mr. Frank Stevens, of Oysterville, nearly lost his life from exposure, having been cast away in a storm on the bay. He had got ashore from the wreck, and was found insensible, on Wednesday afternoon, and it required great exertions to bring him to consciousness. He is rapidly improving.

May 9, 1880 DA

The story about one of the Aberdeen Packing company's fishermen swimming two miles and getting ashore with his clothing on, has been corroborated. It is a fact. The boat was two miles from shore when she capsized, and the anchor falling out, anchored the boat where it went over. The man whose name we cannot ascertain, started for shore, and got in near the Wallicut and lived. His partner was drowned.

May 14, 1880 WA

On the effect of alcohol on the loss of the lives of fishermen, one correspondent to the newspaper said: ...Sleepiness (caused in part by the use of liquors) is the most prolific cause of fatal casualties to fishermen. How many times have you old fishermen seen a boat drifting out toward the bar and not a man to be seen in her? Was it not because they were asleep in the bottom of the boat?

May 14, 1880 WA

Cook's fishing boat, *No. 23*, and the net was picked up yesterday in the vicinity of Sand Island, and it is feared that the captain and his assistant are lost. The captain of this boat was Mr. Andrew Gill, one of the oldest and most reliable fishermen on the river. We hope that the fears respecting his loss may prove to be unfounded. His parents and wife live in this city.

May 14, 1880 WA

Promptings for the sake of humanity would seem to suggest that there should be a signal station at Astoria to give fishermen warning of approaching storms, if for no other purpose.

May 14, 1880 WA

Mr. J. L. Stout, of Ocean View, three miles north of Ilwaco, reported the finding of the body of a man in the surf, half a mile south of his house. An inquest was held and the jury returned a verdict of death by accidental drowning. The age of the person was supposed to be between forty and fifty years, and appeared to have been in the water about three weeks. The description is as follow: length of corpse: five feet ten inches, with large mustache, small goatee, high forehead, small ears, having on an oil coat, heavy blue flannel shirt, black pilot cloth coat, broad striped undershirt, light flannel shirt with various colored stripes, two pairs overalls, blue and brown, No. eight gum boots, heavy flannel scarf around the neck with stripes of three or four colors. In the pockets were found a knife with two blades, point of large one broken and a copper piece of French coin. The body was given Christian burial about one-half a mile south of the residence of Mr. J. L. Stout. After the ceremony, it was resolved that J. D. Holman be appointed to report the facts as above to THE ASTORIAN. The coin, knife and scarf may be seen at the house of Mr. Holman at Ilwaco.

May 26, 1880 DA

Watson's *No. 10* boat was capsized Saturday, but the men were not drowned as reported. They returned to the city yesterday, and we are informed both boat and net were saved. One of the men had a very close call; he was entangled in the net about fifteen minutes.

May 26, 1880 DA

Information is wanted of a young man named Morrison. His father, Captain John B. Morrison of Oakland, Alameda county, California, formerly in Simpson Bro's employment, writes to say that his son left San Francisco to go fishing. He was in Astoria two weeks before the late storm when so many fishermen were drowned. Since then he has not been heard from and his father and mother are very anxious to ascertain if he be alive or not. If any one can give any information, they will confer a favor to him by leaving word at *THE DAILY ASTORIAN.*

May 26, 1880 DA

In reply to an item published in THE DAILY ASTORIAN of Wednesday last, concerning the whereabouts of a son of Capt. John B. Morrison of Oakland, Cal., we have received the following note from J.O. Spencer, of Clifton, Oregon: "Donald Morrison was here from the 17th to the 20th of May and said he was pulling boat in Astoria at the time of the storm. His partner was drowned, and he was saved by the *Rip Van Winkle.* He left here on the 20th for Knappa, Oregon, expecting to find work in a logging camp. He was satisfied with his fishing experience and didn't wish to continue. Have not heard of him since. He may be the one Capt. Morrison of Oakland, Cal, is inquiring about; if so, he is alive and apparently in good health.

May 28, 1880 DA

Who Will Bury the Dead?

The following communication has been handed to us for publication. If the facts are as therein stated, it seems to us that any resident along the weather beach or the river shore line finding a corpse ought immediately after finding it to do as was done in the case of the dead man found near Mr. J. L. Stout's residence, on the weather beach, as reported a few days ago in THE ASTORIAN,— hold an inquest, even if it is an informal one, for the purpose of identifying the corpse, if possible and then give it a decent burial and make public the facts.

ASTORIA, May 27, 1880.

EDITOR ASTORIAN:

We would like to call your attention and the attention of this community to the following facts: You will remember reporting the fact of one of the fishermen of the Aberdeen Packing company and his boat puller being capsized in the late storm, and of the boat puller being drowned and the fisherman swimming some two miles and landing on Sweeney's beach in Washington territory. Now, what we wish to call your attention to is this fact: That the body of the dead boat puller of that boat washed up on the beach a few hundred yards from Sweeney's house on the 14th day of this month, thirteen days ago, and still remains there decomposing in the sun, and food for carrion birds. I would ask you is this a Christian land? One of the proprietors of the cannery for which he was working knows of the body being there, and has said that the company had no time to give the body burial. We simply ask for this space in your valuable columns, so that some one who has a Christian heart in that section of the country may read it and go and perform the last sad rites for one whose parents and kindred are all in a distant land. NEMO.

May 29, 1880 DA

Death in the Breakers.

Mr. J. Kelley, an intimate friend of the late Louis C. Webber, informs us that we were in error in stating that Webber, who in THE ASTORIAN reported drowned on Thursday last, was a German. He informs us that Webber was born in Baltimore, was of Irish descent, and a shoemaker by trade. He has lived a long time in Portland and wore on his vest to his death, a badge of his membership in Wallamet engine company No. 1, of Portland. Webber was lately working at his trade in Leinenweber and Co.'s boot and shoe factory at upper Astoria, but had quit that employment to take his chances of making more money at fishing during the salmon season. On Thursday morning last, he and Tom Johnson, who fished with him for A. Booth & Co.'s cannery, drifted down with the tide with their net out until they had reached a point in the north channel a considerable distance beyond the cape, far out on the bar, and near the western curve of the middle sands. They allowed the net to drift on out, expecting the turn of the tide to drift it back toward them, and then, as usual, they would commence to take up and remove the salmon to the boat. At about 10:45 A.M., Thursday, the 27th inst., Webber being at the tiller and Johnson handling the net, the latter suddenly exclaimed: "Louis, we must get out of this, the fish are striking." (The salmon, touching and striking the ground and their struggling causing a peculiar tugging at the net, showed Johnson that they were getting into shoal water. They were then in about three fathoms.) Webber said "Oh, let her stop here." Almost immediately after, they heard a low moaning noise, and Webber sung out to his companion, who had let go of his net and seized his oars, "head her for the breaker!" which by this time had assumed shape and was rapidly nearing their boat, gaining in size and strength, and rapidity as it approached. In attempting to turn the boat to the now coming breaker that she might meet it head on, one of the oars broke in Johnson's hands, and the remorseless wave struck the broadside of the boat, lifting it on to its crest, turning it over and over as if it had been a cork, leaving both men to struggle for life's breath in the seething waters. Webber was washed out first. Johnson tried to maintain his hold of the boat, but, owing to its rotary motion, he was compelled to let go. The breaker having spent its force, the surface of the water to which both men had arisen, became comparatively smooth. Johnson is a good swimmer, and on looking around, he saw Webber also struggling above water near enough to hear him exclaim, "Tom for God's sake, save me!" He answered, "I will, Louis." Johnson had by this time succeeded in divesting himself of his heavy flannel shirts and was trying to remove his long gum boots which he found a more difficult task. He could do nothing toward saving his companion with these on. He then saw the boom they used for their sail floating toward Webber and told him to seize it, and soon one of the Columbia Canning Co.'s boats (which was making toward them) would pick him up. This boat soon reached Johnson, but he told the men in it not to mind him but to go for Louis who was further in the breakers than he was. Just then the second heavy breaker was fast coming, rolling relentlessly along toward the struggling man, and it would have been at the risk of almost certain death to themselves had the new comers approached the spot nearer. They would only wait to see if the poor fellow would be allowed one more chance for his life after being engulfed the second time. They could do nothing more just then. They saw the cruel wave near its crested head, and drawing the now helpless man in with the undertow, it lifted him up and then broke over him. After this they saw him no more, and it is probable that that is the last of Louis C. Webber until "the sea shall give up the dead that are in it." Johnson was picked up by the men in the Columbia Canning company's boat and with their assistance, he recovered both his boat and net. From the latter they took between seventy and eighty salmon, forty of which he turned over to the men who had aided him in recovering the property and saving his life.

Mr. Webber had been married but a few short months and the sincere sympathy of the community is extended to the widow in her sad bereavement.

May 30, 1880 DA

The body of a drowned man was found floating near the Farmers dock yesterday, by Capt. Phil Johnson. It was conveyed to the undertakers where Coroner Turlay held an inquest on the body which was identified as that of John Francis, a Russian Fin, aged about forty years. The inquest not being concluded we have no further particulars.

June 3, 1880 DA

The Coroner's jury summoned to inquire into the cause of the death of John Francis, whose body was found near the Farmer's dock, after a session lasting nearly all of yesterday, found a majority verdict that the deceased came to his death by violence at the hands of some person or persons to them unknown.

June 4, 1880 DA

Arrested for Murder.

Yesterday morning Chief of Police Barry and Officer Murphy arrested John Christiansen and Lawrence Larsen at the cannery of Badollet & Co., on suspicion of being the murderers of John Francis, whose corpse was found in the river near the Farmers dock on Wednesday last. As the preliminary examination of the prisoners will be held to-day, we forbear mentioning any of the particulars which have led to the arrest of the persons named.

June 4, 1880 DA

There was not enough evidence against them and the two men were released.

In reference to the statement that the bodies of fishermen, drowned during the late gale, had been cast upon Chinook point by the waves and were being torn to pieces by the vultures and gulls, the *Portland Bee* says Mr. Leinenweber, of Astoria, makes the following explanation: "A fisherman, belonging to the Aberdeen Packing company was washed overboard and drowned. In course of time the body came ashore about fifteen miles from Astoria, on the Washington territory side. Word was sent to the Aberdeen company that the body of one of their men had been washed ashore, and a request that it be given decent burial. The answer from the company was that they had no time to attend to the matter. In consequence the body lay for some time exposed to the elements and ravages of the vultures, as stated. The body was on the Washington territory shore, outside of the jurisdiction of the Clatsop county coroner and far from the people of Astoria, and no blame can be attached to them. The Aberdeen Packing company alone are to blame for the outrageous affair, and such inhumanity is deserving of severe condemnation.

June 6, 1880 DA

B.A. Seaborg was the Finnish owner and manager of the Aberdeen Packing Company.

The body of an unknown man was found floating in the river yesterday morning, and was picked up by the steamer *Canby* which brought it ashore, and the remains were conveyed to Franklin's undertaker's shop. It had evidently been in the water a long time as the features were unrecognizable. In a wallet found in his pocket was found a Big Rapid, Michigan hospital certificate containing the name of Leander Matson.

June 8, 1880 DA

A little boy aged seven or eight years, a son of a Russian-Finn named Grinnell, was accidentally drowned in the Nehalem river at Mishawaka, on the 3d instant. It is the first death in that settlement for fourteen years.

June 10, 1880 DA

He was Joseph, son of Britta and Joseph Gronnell.

It is more than probable that two more fishermen lost their lives yesterday morning. Drayman, who was saved by the *Mary Taylor*, asserts that he saw a light in another boat about an hour before daylight. The last he saw of it was close to the whistling buoy, that shortly afterwards the bar began breaking heavily and they must have drifted, he says, where no power on earth could save them.

June 11, 1880 DA

It is our sad duty to announce that two more have been added to the already long list of drowned fishermen this year. Mr. A.T. Brakke, of the Fishermen's Packing company, informs us that Thomas Bell and his boat puller, Charles Williams went out on Tuesday afternoon and have not been seen since. Yesterday Frank Johnson brought up their boat, which belonged to Mr. Brakke, in a wrecked condition. It had been picked up by Mr. Smith off Fort Stevens with nothing whatever in it, and there is but the shadow of a doubt that the unfortunate men are lost. Bell was a steady, sober man, much respected and one of the best fishermen on the river. Rumors of other fishing disasters are afloat, which we hope will not prove true. Thomas Sands and his brother, fishing for the Fishermen's Packing company went out on Tuesday, same time as Bell and Williams, and had not reported up to Friday evening.

June 12, 1880 DA

Early morning as Capt. Deshon, of the *Mary Taylor*, was going out over the bar with building material and supplies for Tillamook rock, he saw two fishing boats fast drifting, in spite of every effort put forth by the men in them, into the breakers. With commendable promptitude, he went to their relief, and not a moment too soon to save four men's lives, he succeeded in throwing them a line and towing them out of the jaws of death. Leonard Drayman, one of the men saved, desirous of expressing his gratitude called at our office and requested the insertion of the card of thanks to Capt. Deshon, which appears in another place. From him we obtained the following particulars. He and Chas. Stone fish for Geo. W. Hume. About half past five yesterday morning, they got caught in the strong ebb tide at the mouth of the river, and in spite of all their efforts they drifted out about two miles beyond the wreck of the *Great Republic*, and had it not been for Capt. Deshon, they and Dick Doyle, with another boat, must inevitably have been capsized and perished in the breakers. Drayman says that he believes that there must have been a sixteen knot current at the time for they had their sail set, fair wind and stiff breeze at that, anchor out with thirty fathom line, and they pulling with all their might and yet they could not stem the current. It is a mystery to us how it is that fishermen persist in placing themselves and their boats in a situation where they have to run such desperate chances, with only a chance of making a few dollars more than those who prefer to be on the safe side.

June 13, 1880 DA

The body of another drowned man washed ashore at fort Stevens yesterday just as the tug was leaving. Dr. Baker informs us it had the appearance of having been in the water but a short time. On one arm was stamped three letters. A coroner was sent for and the body awaiting an inquest when the steamer left.

June 17, 1880 DA

The Lost Fishermen

Mr. Weber furnishes the following list of men lost by the storms of the past season from the Columbia river fishing fleet.

DURING STORM.

- Thomas Gill and George Adams, G.W. Hume's boat *No. 11.*
- Mr. Gadway and net tender, fished for Astoria Fishery or large Kinney cannery.
- Peter J. Blegan and boat puller, Independent.
- Andrew Hansen, fished for G.W. Hume.
- Henry Heinsen, died May 4th in a boat on Chinook beach, after drifting about in a swamped boat eight hours.
- August Wrentz and Dick Jones fished for J.G. Megler and company. Wrentz found entangled in net in boat in the Chinook river.
- Charles Harvey, found on May 12th. Coroners inquest on the 13th. Fished for J.G. Megler & Co. with a man named Pike.
- Alex. Pholson, drowned May 3d or 4th. Fished for the Anglo American packing company with Mr. Johnson, boat *No. 23.*
- Andrew Gill and Alex. Chase, have not the date.
- Thomas Bell and Chas Williams lost about the 8th of June, 1880.
- Thomas F. Sands and Martin Sands lost June 8th, 1880.
- Fred Green and Thomas Dempsey, lost June 10th or 11th. Fished for J.G. Megler and company.
- Lewis Webber, drowned May 27th. Fished at Eagle cannery. Aug. 22, 1880 DA

One Hundred Dollars Reward.

The Hon. A.R. Burbank, of Lafayette, whose daughter, Eva, was lost in the surf off the beach beyond Ilwaco on the 15th while bathing, is there now and is making every possible endeavor to secure the body, and he has authorized THE ASTORIAN to offer a reward of one hundred dollars for the discovery of the remains.

Aug. 22, 1880 DA

The Fatal Bar.

HUNDREDS OF SALMON FISHERMEN DROWNED THIS SEASON.

Columbia River Fisheries How Salmon are Caught and How Men Fish — The Chinese Element Etc.

San Francisco Chronicle, Sept. 4. 1880.

The business of fishing for salmon on the Columbia river is a very dangerous one, if the fishermen just returned from the canneries speak the truth. Some assume that as many as 350 fishermen lost their lives this season on the Columbia. The lowest estimate is furnished by William Johnson who puts the number of victims at 200. Thomas McKenna, alias "Brocky Tom No. 1," states that 250 fishermen were lost. Antone Bereta figures up the list of unfortunates at 300, while Stephen Ellis places it at 350. Ellis has fished for years on the

Columbia. He has been employed at times by the fish commissioner to hatch out young salmon, and is regarded as an authority in piscatorial affairs. He states that the last season on the Columbia was a most disastrous one to all interested in it. The catching of fish commenced several weeks later than usual, and in consequence the canneries discharged the majority of their hands late in July.

The Fish Came up from the Sea

In such numbers that in the hyperbole of Ellis, "you could walk across the river on 'em. Hevins the wather was shtiff wid 'em" A strike of the fishermen seriously complicated matters, [?] that the canneries were totally unprepared to dispose of the great quantities of salmon taken. There was only a few weeks of the season left, and the hands could not be collected in time. The result was that thousands of fish were left to rot on the wharves until the overworked cannerymen found time to throw them back into the river. The fishermen could only dispose of a limited supply, so that at the height of the season, which they had hoped to prove a harvest, they were forced to remain idle. An hours work, sometimes fifteen minutes, supplied them with all the fish they could sell. One cast of the net actually brought up 700 salmon ranging from fifteen to 60 pounds and sufficient to load several boats. It was nothing unusual to throw back numbers of them into the stream and let them pursue their headlong way to the spawning grounds. Ellis, who has fished in various parts of the world and whose most distant recollections are of boats and nets says that he never saw anything like it.

Prodigious Run of Salmon

Both in their number and weight, nets used were 8 1/2 and 8 3/4 inches in the mesh, so that a ten pound salmon could pass through without a moment's hesitation.

Over thirty million pounds of fish were nevertheless taken from April 1st to July 31st when the season closed. During the season of abundance few lives were lost, as there was no necessity to take any risks. Fish could be found in all parts of the stream. It was during the early part of the last season, when salmon were scarce, that the uneasy bar swallowed up its daily sacrifice. A few weeks of warm weather sent the snows into the Columbia in torrents and the great river rushed down to the ocean, swollen and turbulent. Great tracts were inundated and the tides affected. The latter disturbance of Nature was what proved fatal to the fishermen. They watch the tides carefully for at slack water the fish are easiest caught. Leaving their stations on the ebb tide, they shoot out their huge seines, 300 and 350 fathoms in length and drift down the river to be floated back on the flood. It is an important matter with them to know exactly when the tide shall turn.

The Best Fishing Ground

Is close to the bar, and they want to venture no farther. This year the tide table was not to be relied on. The great body of water thrown by the Columbia into the ocean delayed the floods, so that the fishermen were sometimes half an hour and an hour ahead of time. Believing that they were on the last of the ebb, they drifted down and found themselves close to the bar in a tide rushing

41

out at the rate of eight knots an hour. To pull their heavy twenty-four foot boats against such a current was a feat few of them were capable of, and the only course open to the majority was to face death with fortitude. Others perished from the desire of gain. Some fishermen having a heavy boat would venture out on dangerous waters and return with a great catch of fish. Next day, others who had toiled for days, perhaps, with indifferent success, would follow the bad example, to be heard of no more. The majority of the fishermen are old sailors, and with the recklessness of their class, are disposed to

Take Desperate Chances.

This spirit of emulation proved fatal to many. Some fisherman, anxious to display his seamanship and bravery, would venture out farther than was safe. Some other aspirant for a small degree of fame along the wharves at Astoria would go still farther, and so the contest would proceed, until several canneries would be minus boats and nets. The majority, however, perished through fatal mistakes with regard to the tides. The great storm on the 2d of May swelled the list of casualties to an alarming size. Johnson and Ellis happened to be up the stream some distance; McKenna and Beretta were, however, close to the bar. The Italian, after a sharp run for his life, escaped to the shore, but McKenna was swept over the bar. Finding himself in the jaws of death, he seized the only chance left him, and in his open boat, stood straight out to sea. By this means he escaped immediate death, but nearly died of starvation, as he was three days outside the bar without food. He has fished for many years on the Columbia, but he says, "I've done with it; it's too risky for me." He asserts that in that memorable gale,

Sixty Men Were Lost.

"The cannery men," he assured a Chronicle reporter, "never report half the men lost. "All they care for is to get the boats back, and if they do, it's all right. If they don't, what's the good of ever talking about it. It won't get them the boat and it may keep away fishermen next year." This view to the matter is shared by Johnson, Ellis and Beretta. "Of course," said Ellis, "Tom ought to know better than I do how many men were drowned that night on the bar, for he was there, but the talk all along the river was that there were a hundred lost." The estimates of the fishermen may be exaggerated. It is characteristic of this class to treat figures in a very reckless manner, but the evidence is strong that numbers of accidents occurred on the Columbia that were never reported. Even placing the losses at 150, which is far below the lowest estimate furnished by the fishermen, the sacrifice of life is fearful. The cannery people say that they have no interest to subserve in suppressing the reports to accidents, and give all the information asked. Admitting this statement to be perfectly true, it is quite possible for the fishermen's stories to be correct. The official report of 1878-9 gives the number of boats belonging to the canneries at 800. There are over

Fourteen Hundred Boats Engaged

On the Columbia—some say sixteen hundred. Many farmers have several boats; and other parties own their own crafts and supply salmon to the canneries. Of this private fleet, the canneries know little, and are certainly not under any obligations to keep a watchful eye on other people's employes with a view to furnish them to the newspapers. The terrors of poverty, as well as of tide and storm, hung over the unfortunate fishermen this year. Many of them were unable to pay their board bills. Usually they clear a few hundred dollars to fortify them against the winter. The price of a fish is fifty cents, of which the cannery retains one-third for supplying the boat and net, valued at $625. The thirty-five canneries on the Columbia river employ about 4,000 Chinamen in preparing fish for market. It is safe to say that, were the work done by white hands, there would be employment for 2,000 girls and boys labeling cans and other light work. The Chinese get thirty dollars a month, and are growing so independent that they struck several times this year for higher wages, and, on different occasions, offered violence to their employers. They never venture on the river for the fishermen are not the class to tamely submit to such competition. Some years ago a few

Adventurous Mongolians

Joined the fleet, but they disappeared the same night. Their boats were broken to pieces, and their nets cut up and scattered on the beach. The fishermen made no attempt to conceal the fact that they had drowned the intruders, and the authorities never investigated it. The work would have been idle. Since then, the white fishermen have had the field to themselves. As before stated, they explore it with a great net, 300 fathoms or 1,800 feet in length. The top of the net is supported by corks, the bottom weighed down with lead. When no obstuctions are encountered, the net drifts along evenly with the tide, and the moment the fish strike it and ensnare themselves, it is hauled in. The fishermen can tell by the corks where the captives are struggling, and he hauls in that part only. Sometimes, however, a great school of freshly run salmon, mad to reach the headwaters, dash against the whole length of the net, and then comes the tug of war. In dull times when the salmon are scarce the fisherman has his patience sorely tried by the seals who will watch the net as carefully as he does himself, and rob it before his eyes.

The Seal

Has a weakness for the jowl of the salmon, and will offer his epicurean palate only that portion. Having taken one bit of the fish he tosses it contemptuously aside, and in this manner will destroy twenty salmon before the indignant fisherman can intercept him. Having had ample opportunity to observe the habits of the seal family, the Columbia river fishermen confidently denounce the tribe as the arch enemies of the finny race, and laugh at the idea that the sea-lions at the mouth of the harbor are harmless. To the salmon the seals are particularly deadly, for the king of fishes rushes from the sea blind to all obstacles, and falls an easy prey to the wiley phocacean, waiting for him in midwater. Sometimes, retributive justice overtakes the robber, and the fishermen hauling in his share finds the dark corpse of his enemy rolled up in the net. The ponderous and stupid sturgeon is another pest of the patient fisherman. Nodding in his boat, he sees the cork go whizzing under the water, and with great labor drags up the miles of twine and pounds of lead, only to find a worthless monster that has to be cut loose. Sturgeon on the Columbia in the salmon season are not considered worth the trouble of towing ashore. These troubles of the fishermen, are, however but the trivial annoyances that assist in making the sum total of the life that is supported by the sweat of his brow. The great misery of his existence is the fear that any tide may sweep him to destruction, and the foregoing statements of unimpeached witnesses show that this dread is anything but groundless.

September 10, 1880 DA
It was the opinion of the editor of the Daily Astorian, at the time, that these numbers were greatly exaggerated.

The sudden death of Mr. H.T. Dennis of John Day, on Saturday last, is a matter of sincere regret. He was beloved by all. He had been on the streets of the city an hour before his death, in apparent health, and took the mail from the postoffice for Fernhill, and some purchases which he had made at the stores, and started homeward in his boat. The boat was picked up afloat in the bay that evening about nine o'clock, and poor Henry Dennis was found in it a corpse. An examination before the coroner revealed the facts that his death was caused by heart disease. He leaves an aged mother, a sister and a brother, and numerous friends, to mourn his sudden departure. The funeral was attended in this city yesterday.

Sept. 24, 1880 DA

Mr. E. C. Jeffers of Prospect hill was caught in all the fury of the storm yesterday forenoon about midway from the mouth of Lewis and Clark and Smith point. He lost sail, sprit, etc., the boat shipped heavy seas, half filled and all together it was a very close call. He says the rain poured down like as if it was a water-spout. We are sincerely grateful that his mishaps were no worse. We dislike to write the obituary notice of such genial friends as him.

Sept. 24, 1880 DA

A fisherman's boat capsized in the bay yesterday, but the men hung to the keel and were finally rescued, and the boat towed into safety at upper Astoria.

April 6, 1881 DA

The body of a man, supposed to be a fisherman, washed up on the weather beach opposite Skipanon and was found July 4th. No particulars.

July 9, 1881 DA

Child Drowned.

My youngest son, four years old, blue eyes, light hair and complexion, fell from the wharf at Clifton on Saturday morning, July 9th, 1881. A liberal reward will be paid for the recovery of his body.

VINCENT COOK
Clifton, Oregon, July 10, 1881

Grief-Stricken

A severe, piercing, and bitter grief has overtaken the family of our friend Vin Cook, Esq., at Clifton. Their little son, Ralph Nesmith, was drowned off

44

the wharf there Saturday. Diligent search has been made for the body; the river dragged, giant powder exploded, etc., but still the water refuses to give up its dead. Our tenderest sympathies are expressed for them in their sadness. Mr. Spencer, in a note to THE ASTORIAN, says: "Ralph was four years and four months old. A brighter or more affectionate boy never lived; was all you could wish for a boy of his age; and his loss falls heavily on all of us."

July 12, 1881 DA

Body Found.

To the Hon. J.Q.A. Bowlby, Judge of County court of Clatsop county, Oregon.

Having been notified this day of a dead body washed ashore on Clatsop beach, near Mr. P. Condits place, I went to said place and found the dead body of a man of the following description: Height, six feet, fair complexion, light hair and a light mustache. He had four shirts on, one heavy red woolen over-shirt, one check over-shirt, one new white shirt and one blue flannel under-shirt, one pair blue flannel under-shirt, one pair blue flannel drawers, a pair cassimere pants, dark plaid, a pair of No. 9 shoes buckled on the side, and a pair of woolen socks, no marks of any description on the body, and nothing in the pockets of his clothes. I had a coffin made and took the body around up on the sand ridge, back of Mr. West's farm, and buried it, placed a board at the grave and marked it unknown. The expenses incurred are: Coroners fees, $5 00; mileage, six miles and return, $1 20; for coffin, $2 00; for burying, $1 50; for team to haul body up from the beach, $5 00. All of which I respectfully submit to the County court.

JOHN ELLIS,
Ex Officio Justice of the Peace
And Acting Coroner.   July 6, 1881

July 19, 1881 DA

A little child of W. H. Twilight fell off the street into the bay yesterday. It was rescued by Mr. C.W. Stone, just in the nick of time.

July 20, 1881 DA

One of the sailors coming down on the *Lurline* yesterday to join his ship, the *Invercargil*, fell overboard while passing Columbia city. The steamer immediately turned back and rescued the man none the worse for his ducking. Cause, too much whiskey. There seems to be a special providence for drunken men.

Sept. 4, 1881 DA

Last Friday afternoon, Chas. Savage left Knappa in a skiff, where he had been on a hunting expedition, and when almost abreast of Tongue Point and in the middle of the river, his skiff capsized, leaving him struggling in the water. He struck out for the shore when a passing plunger rescued him. He says he never could have reached the shore, as he was becoming numbed and exhausted, but for the timely arrival of the plunger.

Oct. 16, 1881 DA

Found Drowned.

As the steamer *Willamette Chief* was backing from the ship below the O.R. & N. Co.'s dock yesterday noon, the tide being low, the dead body of a man appeared which had been evidently in the water for a long time. The remains were conveyed to Coroner Franklin's undertaking rooms and a jury summoned. The verdict was that the body was that of J. J. Brien, whose mysterious disappearance was noted in this paper about four weeks ago. He was a former resident of this place, but of late had been living in Portland, where he has friends and relatives. They were notified by telegraph last evening.

Feb. 25, 1882 DA

Body Found

Skipanon May 19, 1882
EDITOR ASTORIAN:

I herewith give you an account of a man on Clatsop beach about 8 miles south of Skipanon landing. Said body wore one white shirt, one coarse gray woolen shirt, one pair coarse cotton drawers, one pair blue overalls, 1 pair duck overalls, black vest, faded black beaver coat, southwester and oil skin coat. Personal description about 54 inches high *[5 feet 4 inches]*, well built, fine black hair, light mustasche. In pocket were found some white rags, a red silk handkerchief with J. Richten marked in one corner, a copy of the DAILY ASTORIAN of April 22, a ring with a small key, a white handled 3 bladed pocket knife, a pocket comb, 1 beer ticket from Ginder, a tide table for April, half dollar U.S. coin., 1 Bavarian 3 kreutzer piece of 1851 vintage, a cannery ticket marked A. Booth, No. 66, April 22d, boat *No. 22*, No. of fish 4.

Owing to an advanced state of decomposition, it was buried as decently as circumstances would permit.

For the above articles and further information, address
J.L. LEVERSON,
Skipanon, Oregon

May 20, 1882 DA

Body Found

Peterson's Point, W.T. *Washington Territory*

September 15, 1882
EDITOR ASTORIAN:

To-day there was found on the beach near Gray's Harbor, the body of a man supposed to be the remains of one of the men who were drowned when the *Gen. Miles* was coming here on the 26th ult. The corpse looked as though it had been in the water two or three weeks. The deceased was six feet in height, large in proportion, had on white shirt, small studs in bosom, dark pants, double-breasted dark vest, nice striped overshirt and blue blanket shirt, large heavy tongue-leather boots, red handkerchief in hip pocket, buckskin money purse in vest pocket containing four silver trade dollars, and one metal watch box. He had a bald head, sandy complexion and heavy sandy moustache. I had as good a box made as could be under the circumstances, and gave

46

the body decent burial on the beach above high water. No doubt the friends of deceased will be glad to know that the body has come ashore.

GLENN PETERSON
Sept. 21, 1882 DA

The body of an unknown man was picked up in the river yesterday afternoon, a short distance below Tongue Point, and brought to the coroner's for identification. It is believed to be the body of Peter George who drowned at Clifton about a month ago.

May 6, 1883 DA

Drowning of Walter Pohl

At a quarter to three yesterday morning the tug *Pioneer* was going out the south channel; Captain Bochau was on the bridge, Pilot Campbell on the house just in front, and Walter Pohl at the wheel. The breakers were coming in rough, and the captain told him to hold her with her head to the sea. He turned his back for an instant, and when he looked around Pohl was gone. The supposition is that as the boat struck a heavy sea, the rudder straightened suddenly, causing the wheel to "kick," and throwing the poor fellow over with lightning rapidity. The whole thing happened in less time than it takes to write it, and for some seconds, Capt. Bochau couldn't realize that his nephew, who had but a moment before been standing almost at his side, was hurled to a violent death. To put the tug about was impossible, and the dim light of the moon also made it impossible to distinguish any object in the water. There was no help or hope. The body has not been recovered, nor is it likely it will be. Deceased was in his twenty-second year; a fine hearty young man, the oldest son of Mrs. Pohl, of this city, the sudden death of whose brother, Chas. Bochau, occurred last Tuesday. The double loss of brother and son, by sudden death inside of a week is a terrible blow to the mother who has the sympathy of the entire community.

Yesterday afternoon the flags were at half mast on the tugs, and at the lodge of the I.O.O.F., which order the deceased had joined about three weeks ago. A reward of $50 is offered for the recovery of the body.

May 22, 1883 DA

Found Drowned

At an early hour last Sunday morning, the body of John Martin was seen in the water near Jas. Magee's house above Jno. Devlin's cannery. The body was brought ashore and yesterday the coroner held an inquest with the following result.

Coroner's Inquest

In the matter of the inquisition upon the body of John Martin, deceased, we the undersigned jurors summoned to appear before B.B. Franklin, coroner of the precinct of Astoria, county and state aforesaid, at the undertaking rooms in the City of Astoria, Ogn, on the 4th day of June, 1883, to inquire into the cause of the death of the said John Martin, having been duly sworn according to law, and having made such inquisition after inspecting the body and hearing

47

the testimony, adduced upon our oaths, each and all do say that we do find the deceased was named John Martin, was a native of —— —— [left blank], aged about 35 years, that he came to his death on the 2nd day of June, 1883, by accidental drowning in the Columbia river near J.A. Devlin's cannery in this city, while in a state of intoxication. And we further find deceased had on his person the sum of $18.80. All of which we duly certify to by this inquisition in writing. By us signed this 4th day of June, 1883.

CHAS. S. WRIGHT, Foreman	THOS. LOGAN
L.E. SELIG	R.F. WILLIAMS
A.M. BEEDE	F.C. NORRIS

June 5, 1883 DA

Drowning of H.A. Parker

Hazen A. Parker was drowned between the dock and the steamer *Clara Parker* at one o'clock yesterday morning. Deceased was a native of Vermont, in the 44th year of his age. He was a machinist by trade, but of late had been employed as fireman on the *Clara Parker*. At the hour mentioned yesterday morning, he started to go aboard the boat, but missing his footing fell into the water. His cries attracted the attention of someone on board who flung him a rope, but being unable to grasp it, he was drowned. Parties were engaged yesterday in grappling for the body, but up to last evening all efforts were unsuccessful. H.B. Parker offers a reward of $25 for the body.

June 13, 1883 DA

Drowned in the Walluski
Found Dead Among the Logs

On the Walluski, about six miles from Astoria, and about two miles from where that stream empties into Young's Bay, Frank Johnson and Albert Nash have had a logging camp for some time past, and have been building a boom during the past week. Friday morning Nash went down to the landing to put in a boom stick, and was last seen at 2 o'clock in the afternoon. Not returning that night, some of the employes went to look for the missing man, and at an early hour yesterday morning, the body was found jammed in among the logs and a gash in his right forehead. He had been dead some hours. The body was brought to town yesterday morning, and the circumstances being so clearly stated it was deemed unnecessary to hold an inquest. The funeral will take place this afternoon from Coroner Franklin's undertaking rooms.

Nash was a large powerfully built man weighing 195 pounds, and was well liked by his acquaintances. He came here from California some years ago, and has three sisters living in Missouri, of which state he was a native. He was 33 years of age and unmarried.

Nov. 18, 1883 DA

The skies that flush in crimson splendor above the fir-crowned hills were radiant yesterday with the rose and purple tints of May; the white sails of the river fleet glittered in sunshine and dimmed in shadow on the water. Nature in all her pride of pomp and pageantry wore the brightest tinted robes of the joyous spring time, and DeForce began smashing salmon heads at his oil works on Youngs river.

May 8, 1884 DMA

The boats that went ashore at Sand Island last Monday were boat 42 of J.W. & V. Cook. Thos. Hunter, the captain was saved by Capt. Al Harris. Fred Randenbaum, the boat puller, aged 19, a native of Lubeck, Germany, was drowned. Boat *22*, of J. O. Hanthorn, had in it John Gregor, captain, who was saved and T. Russell, boat puller, who was drowned. The sad death list of the poor fellows who are caught in the breakers is fully up to that of former seasons.

May 8, 1884 DMA

Drowned at Upper Astoria

Last Sunday morning, Jas. A. Bell, Jr. with his brother, Thomas, brought their horses to the river beach near their home at upper Astoria. In some way, one of the horses reared, throwing his rider into the water. His brother, Thos., went to his assistance as did Mr. Thomes, but unfortunately, it was found impossible to save him. The body was recovered in a short time and will be buried at Clatsop cemetery to-day. Deceased, had he lived to next February, would have been twenty-one years of age. The funeral services will take place at ten o'clock this morning at the Swedish church at upper Astoria. A steamboat will be at Badollet & Co.'s cannery to carry the friends and acquaintances of the deceased to the cemetery. Friends of the family are invited to attend.

August 5, 1884 DMA

Lost at Sand Island.

Last Wednesday night about eleven o'clock, Otto Schuring and Olaf Knutsen, in one of Hume's boats, were putting out their net, and in some way the boat capsized. Their cries for help were heard, but before assistance could reach them they were gone. Their dead bodies were found on Peacock spit yesterday morning and brought to this city for burial. They were both young men, Schuring being but 22 years of age, and Knutsen 24, and were well liked by their brother members of the A.W.P.U. Schuring will be buried from the residence of his brother, Andrew, at two o'clock this afternoon. At the same hour, Knutsen's funeral will take place from the same place.

August 5, 1884 DMA

The *Sol R. Thomas* lay alongside Flavel's dock yesterday taking in lumber, Chinamen and supplies for the Bath cannery at Umpqua. The white caps on the green water hissed and broke against the piles, the Chinamen in the stern of the vessel grew pale, and one burned a little punk stick and flung to the wild winds a handful of crimson paper. All sorts of freight, dead and alive, were pushed and hoisted aboard, and the craft swung out to sea. The vessel will be back to-morrow, and on Sunday goes to the Coquille, forty miles further down with ninety Chinamen for the Coquille packing company whose manager, Mr. Getchell, is now in the city.

August 8, 1884 DMA

About the 30th of June, THE ASTORIAN had an item regarding the loss of Sam Blair and Jas Craig who were drowned on the bar. Mr. C.L. Watson, cashier of the First National Bank of Pittston, Pennsylvania, writes asking for information about Jas. Craig. Anyone who knows anything about the unfortunate young man will confer a favor on a grief-stricken family by addressing that gentleman or communicating with Mr. P.L. Cherry, British vice consul, at this place.

August 8, 1884 DMA

Frank Surprenant started from Fort Stevens last Wednesday afternoon in a row boat, but one of his oars breaking, he went drifting toward the bar. The crew of the *Geo. S. Homer* rescued him. It was a narrow escape.

February 20, 1885 DA

Yesterday afternoon, the attention of some men were directed to the dead body of a man floating past Flavel's dock. It was brought into the Cass 10th street dock, and upon examination at Coroner Ross' office was found to be the body of Louis Eckhart. The unfortunate man had been drowned on the 18th of last November, while unloading wood at Hanthorn's cannery. He was a native of Germany, aged 32 years, a member of Castle Lodge, K. of P., No. 62, Red Bluff, California, and will be given decent burial by Astor Lodge, No. 6, K. of P., at 1 o'clock this afternoon.

Feb. 27, 1885 DA

Drowned.

Frank and Eddie Pitkin, sons of S.J. Pitkin, aged 14 and 9 years respectively, started from the beach above Trullinger's mill yesterday morning at nine o'clock in a small row boat. The ebb tide caught them and sent the boat broadside on against the piles under Trullinger's wharf. The boat upset and the boys cried loudly for help as they struggled in the water. Before assistance could possibly reach the unfortunate lads, they were swept below the surface and drowned. Boats immediately put out, and all day long strenuous efforts were made to recover the bodies but without avail. Universal sympathy is felt for the sorrowing parents who were so instantly bereaved of their children.

March 22, 1885 DA

Yesterday afternoon, John Palm who is fishing for the Cutting Packing Company was taking in his drift toward Skipanon when a sea lion swimming up attempted to upset the boat. Palm fought him with an oar but at last reached for his revolver when the phoca *[the scientific name for the seal genus]* gave up the fight as he was not ready to fight a man with a revolver. In attempting to get a shot at the beast, Palm, in his excitement, discharged the weapon, the ball striking and shattering his left wrist.

May 2, 1885 WA

Sad Accident

About half-past nine last Sunday evening, Waldemer, youngest son of Mrs. Eva Wallman, was playing in the rear of his mother's hotel and in some way fell into the water. Though there were three or four men standing by, not one of them seemed to have presence of mind enough to save the poor little fellow and though he could be seen struggling in the water, he was drowned before assistance reached him. His body was recovered yesterday morning and the funeral will take place from the Germania hotel at four o'clock this afternoon. The bereaved mother has the sympathy of the community in the loss of her darling boy.

May 12, 1885 DA

At a late hour last Wednesday night, Fred Holm and his boat puller in boat *No. 6* of the Astoria Packing Company were thrown into the water by the upsetting of their boat on Clatsop spit. The boat puller scrambled into the bottom of the boat; Holm instantly disappeared and was seen no more. In two hours, John Peterson, of boat 7 belonging to the same cannery, who was rowing by, heard the boat puller's cries and at considerable personal risk, saved the man; the boat and net went out over the bar. Holm was a Russian Finn, unmarried aged 30 years.

July 17, 1885 DA

S.B. Osborn writes from his place at Williamsport that at a late hour on the night of Monday, the 13th, John Bushard left Youngs bay intending to go up Young's river. Nothing was further heard or seen of him, but the following day his boat was found bottom upwards opposite J.G. Nurnburg's; his hat was floating on the water. The presumption is that the unfortunate man is drowned.

July 17, 1885 DA

The operator at the Cape reports that at 6:45 last evening the dead body of a man was seen floating out to sea. The only thing that could be distinguished was that the head was bald and the body clothed in black. Some poor unfortunate who may have left some hearthstone desolate.

July 18, 1885 WA

Body Found

It will be remembered that Jno. Bouchard, a man well known in this vicinity, was drowned about nine days ago, while going from J.B. Osborn's place on Young's river, farther east. Yesterday afternoon, F.W. Wass and J.B. Osborn started in a boat to look for the body, and rowing to the spot where his boat and hat had previously been found, they searched among the tules. In a short time, they found the body about sixty yards from the place where he disappeared. Wass came over to town and notified the coroner, who went over last evening to hold an inquest if necessary.

July 22, 1885 DMA

A Terrible Accident.
Drowning of two Men in the Stream Opposite the City

Word came from Knappton yesterday of a dreadful accident that occurred last Tuesday night, resulting in the drowning of two men and the serious injury of a third. The particulars are very meagre and the most diligent inquiry yesterday failed to secure any more than the merest outlines of the occurrence.

It appears that at eight o'clock last Tuesday evening three men left this city in a fishing boat belonging to a man named Fitzpatrick living at Skamokawa, intending to go to that place. When about half way across the river and about opposite Knappton one of the men who was in the bow of the boat suddenly lurched forward and fell overboard. One of his companions who was in the stern steering made a jump to save his comrade and he too fell overboard. At that moment the boom of the sail came round with such force as to partly overturn the boat, the sail fouled and struck the water, the boat capsizing and throwing the remaining man out. About ten o'clock he drifted onshore about a mile and a half below Knappton where he found assistance and was cared for; he was unconscious when picked up and dreadfully bruised. Not till yesterday morning was he able to give any account of the affair and even then was too exhausted to more than give the faintest outlines of the terrible fate that befell his unfortunate companions. To add to the difficulty of getting any information about the matter it appears that the man who was saved was a stranger to the other two men and was simply a passenger. Parties on the *Novelty* heard that a man known as "Boston Bill" was one of the men drowned. The other man is described as being of medium height, dressed in black, carrying a gold watch. The name of the man who got ashore is said to be Frank Hamlin. The boat, battered and stove in, came ashore yesterday morning below where the man had drifted before. Further and more authentic particulars are awaited with anxious interest.

Sept. 12, 1885 WA

A Narrow Escape
Gallant Rescue of Two Men at Ft. Stevens Wharf.

DAILY ASTORIAN FRIDAY

Yesterday afternoon about three o'clock, two men named Vincent and Moody, employed on the government works at Ft. Stevens, rowed alongside one of the rock laden barges lying at the wharf to get aboard. As the boat struck the side of the barge, it upset, throwing the men into the water. They were immediately sucked under the barge, coming to the surface about 100 feet below. The tide was going out like a mill race, and it looked as if there was no help for the men who struck out and battled manfully for their lives, the tide carrying them swiftly down. Mr. Foster and another man leaped into a boat which was hastily lowered from the wharf and went to their assistance. It was a race for life, but the rescuers were equal to it and reached the men before they were entirely exhausted, they being then some three hundred yards below the wharf. In a few moments both were hauled aboard. So great was the force of the tide that it was found impossible to make headway against it, and Foster and his companion landed on the beach about a quarter of a mile below the barge.

This is the first accident that has occurred since the inception of the work and to the promptness of the rescuers the men owe their lives. Some time ago Capt. Powell applied for a boat to be ready for use in just such an emergency, and it is only a few days ago that it was supplied. The davits had not yet been put up by which the boat was to swing, it lying on the upper wharf at the time the men were upset. The boat that they were in at the time drifted rapidly out to sea.

Sept. 12, 1885 WA

FOUND DROWNED

Chris. Johnson Found in the River Near Hanthorn's Cannery.

The body of Chris Johnson, a resident of Alderbrook, was found floating in the river near J.O. Hanthorn's cannery yesterday morning. On the 8th he started to Gray's river to look over some land in that section, returning on the *Union* last Friday. He was last seen alive near Johansen's at upper Astoria, that afternoon. On Monday, his continued absence alarmed his friends and a telegram was sent to Vancouver asking if he was there, to which a reply was received saying that a man answering to the description had been there inquiring about land. This allayed the fears of his family and friends, but yesterday morning at seven o'clock, Messrs. Welcome and Bruen, with R. Johnson, a brother of the missing man, who were at Hanthorn's wharf, saw the drowned body of a man floating in the water between the beach and the roadway. They got a boat and brought the body ashore. The brother recognized it as the body of the missing man.

Coroner Ross held an inquest, the jury finding that the deceased was a native of Denmark, 33 years of age, and came to his death on or about the 11th of September, by accidentally falling into the Columbia river from the roadway at upper Astoria and drowning. Deceased leaves a wife and six children, the youngest being but three days old. The funeral will take place from the Scandinavian church at upper Astoria at one o'clock this afternoon.

Sept. 17, 1885 DA

The body of the little girl found below Knappa last week is said to have been identified as the remains of a nine-year-old girl named Anderson, who was drowned on Blind slough, above Knappa about a year ago.

Oct. 16, 1885 DA

DROWNED AT UPPER TOWN

Jno. Emerson was drowned at upper Astoria about half past five yesterday afternoon under peculiar circumstances. He was standing with three or four other men on the dock of the Fishermen's Packing Co.'s premises when some one called to him that his boat was loose. The boat was only a few yards from shore and the wind was setting it in. There were other boats close by, any one of which could have been apparently used, but he ran to the side of the dock and made a jump, intending to light in his boat and bring it ashore. He missed the boat and fell in the water. He rose and shouted for help, but before assistance could reach him he was drowned. He leaves a wife and two children. Two brothers live in the vicinity of his place near Alderbrook. He was about 35 years of age. The body had not been recovered last evening.

Oct. 16, 1885 DA

Came Ashore

Coroner Ross received a telegram last Sunday evening that a body had come ashore on Clatsop beach. He went down that evening and held an inquest yesterday. The body came ashore near the Seaside house. It was that of a man 38 or 40 years of age; five feet nine inches in height, dark complexion, had on red flannel underwear, gray flannel overshirt and overalls. The verdict was that he was drowned in the ocean. It is believed that he was off the plunger *Emma*, two others manifestly from that unfortunate craft coming ashore last week. The pockets of the deceased were turned inside out and completely rifled, the goulish cupidity of those first discovering the body destroying any probability of the unfortunate man's identification. The burial will be to-day.

Nov. 17, 1885 DA

Fifty Dollars Reward

I WILL PAY THE ABOVE REWARD for the recovery of the body of E. F. Cochran, drowned at Walker's Island on Wednesday the 4th inst. Fell overboard from the steamer R.R. Thompson; about five feet, four inches in height, dark hair and eyes, and mustache, about 50 years old.

K.A. NOYES
Nov. 25, 1885 DA

Drowned at Upper Astoria

A distressing accident occurred at upper Astoria yesterday afternoon, resulting in the drowning of Beni Bell, the nine-year-old son of Jno. A. Bell. The boy, with his brother and a companion named Barnhart, had gone out in a small skiff, and the skiff overturning, threw the three children into the water. The others were saved by parties who hastened to the rescue, but Benny sank before assistance could reach him. The body was recovered last evening. The funeral will take place at eleven o'clock tomorrow morning.

Nov. 27, 1885 DMA

DECENT INTERMENT REQUIRED

CLATSOP, Nov. 21, 1885
EDITOR ASTORIAN:

A word in regard to the manner in which dead bodies cast up on Clatsop beach are disposed of, seems to be called for. The bodies of fishermen and sailors who are drowned at the mouth of the Columbia, as well as farther down the coast, frequently come ashore here. It is customary to have them buried in the sand near the spot where they are picked up, often where the high tides may wash over the graves. These graves usually made very shallow, are frequently washed out leaving the bodies uncovered. The loose sand on those out of reach of the water is often blown away, leaving the grave open. In one case at least the box was left entirely exposed, someone pried it open and the bones of the dead were left to be scattered along the beach.

Burial is intended to serve two purposes: to show proper respect to the dead, and to guard against offense to the living. Such burial as this fails in both, just as well let the bodies rot on the beach and be the food of birds. If it is intended to show respect to the dead, the graves ought at least to be put where they will not be violated. If it is intended to put them out of sight of the living, the bodies should be buried so as to remain out of sight. We should suppose that the cemetery was the proper place to bury the dead.

We would respectfully suggest that the coroner, or whoever has charge of this business, see that this evil be remedied. The careless manner in which these stray bodies are disposed of is an offense, and a nuisance, and a crime against the community.

H.S. LYMAN
Nov. 27, 1885 DA

MORE ABOUT INTERMENT

Astoria, Nov. 27th, 1885.
EDITOR ASTORIAN:

I would like to thank H.S. Lyman for his remarks which I fully endorse.

What is the use of a coroner if he does not attend to the duties of his office, and attend to the burial of those bodies?

But at the same time, the coroner cannot do much when some of the people living along the beach take the law into their own hands, as has been done on several occasions, and the coroner was not notified at all. I remember a case about a year ago. There were two men washed off the *Willamette* while crossing the bar: one of them was a Mason, and the Masonic lodge of Astoria offered a reward of $50 for the recovery of his body. Shortly after, two bodies came ashore on Clatsop beach, and I am satisfied that they were the two men, but instead of notifying the coroner as they should, the finders buried the bodies on the beach, and the coroner knew nothing of it until he saw the account of two bodies being found and buried by some one on Clatsop beach, paying no attention to the published reward, nor caring for the feelings of the friends; not even trying to find out if they had friends or not. I would like to see the law take hold of some of those people.

Another time I know of, a body being found and the coroner being notified; he went to the place with a jury to hold an inquest, and found something over $40 on the body, and then, instead of complying with section 462, chapter 39 of the general laws of Oregon, he caused the body to be buried where it lay, about two feet deep in the sand.

I am very glad some one has called attention to this slack way of doing; it is the duty of every civilized person finding a dead body to report it to the coroner, so that it may be ascertained if possible, who the person was, and all the particulars, so that should the friends, at any future time, wish to claim the remains, they could do so. The county has a piece of ground for the purpose of burying the poor and unknown, and they will not object to the burying of any bodies there that may be found on Clatsop beach. The coroner will always endeavor to do his duty if the people will do their duty in notifying him.

Yours, etc., J.C. Ross

Nov. 28, 1885 DA

FOUR MEN MISSING.
Fears Expressed as to Their Safety.

Last Monday, four men started from here to go to the Wallicut river—Andrew Barry, Oscar Petersen, and two others, Ericson and Johnson. About 11:30, they were abreast of Kinney's cannery, heading across the river. Since that time, they have not been seen and it is feared they have been drowned. The mate of the *Carmaethen Castle* which went to sea last Tuesday, reported that that afternoon a boat went drifting by Sand Island bottom upward with two men clinging on, but that it was too rough to lower a boat to go to their assistance. It is also reported that the boat has come ashore at Ilwaco. A search party will start to look for them this morning and it is thought that some definite intelligence as to their fate will be learned to day.

Dec. 24, 1885 DA

The four men spoken of in yesterday's issue as having been reported drowned are all right, having arrived at their destination in safety. The question now arises whose boat was it that drifted ashore, bottom upward at Ilwaco? It was that that first made surmise that accident had befallen the party that left here for the Wallicut last Monday.

Dec. 25, 1885 DA

Pilot Gunderson reports that while on the *Glengaber* on Christmas eve, about fifty miles west of Cape Hancock, they passed the wreck of a schooner, bottom upward. She was about fifty feet in length; the rudder was gone. There was nothing about the hull to identify. *Dec. 29, 1885 DA*

Last Saturday night, A.J. Brune and O. Anderson, while laying out their net in the ship channel near Harrington Point, heard cries of some one in distress, but supposing the sound to be made by seals, they finished laying out, when they concluded to find out from whence the sound came. Leaving their net in charge of a boat near and pulling in the direction of the sound, a skiff was found capsized and a man clinging to the bottom in a very exhausted condition. The man rescued was an Englishman. He stated that he and his companion, a Norwegian, were capsized while crossing the river and his companion attempted to swim ashore, but was probably drowned. The name of either was not learned.

Oct. 9, 1886 WA

Two men found the dead body of a man lying on the tide flats near John Day's yesterday morning and brought it to town, notifying coroner Ross, who, upon investigation elicited the following facts: The drowned man was a sailor, a native of Norway, aged 25, named Fred Johnson. He came here on the *Balaklava* and while in port was taken sick and sent to the hospital where he remained three weeks. After the *Balaklava* sailed, he recovered and went fishing. On the night of the 2nd inst., while in a boat with his companion near Harrington's point, they started to change places; the boat upset; the other man climbed up on the capsized boat and was rescued by A.J. Brune and O. Anderson. Johnson started to swim ashore, but was drowned, and his body was discovered yesterday. Some wages were due him, but they had been sent to the owners of the *Balaklava* in London. So he will be buried by the county to-day, as many a poor fellow has been before who has lost his life in the waters of the lower Columbia.

Oct. 16, 1886 WA

A terrible accident befell John Keogh, a sailor on board the British bark *Dinapore* last Monday evening, which may result in his death. He was in the rigging and some way fell headlong into the hatchway, striking on his back, and fracturing the spinal vertebrae between the shoulders. He was conveyed to the hospital and surgical attendance summoned. He is but 19 years of age. His pulse last night was 103, and but slight hopes are entertained of his recovery.

Oct. 16, 1886 WA

Capt. A.M. Simpson, who came up from San Francisco on the new tug *Traveler*, tells of a narrow escape he had at Coos bay. When off Coos bay on the way up, the tug started to put in there. The sea was rough and when on the bar, the tug gave a lurch and threw Capt. Simpson overboard. "Heave me a rope," said he as he rose to the surface. But everything had been lashed fast and there was no line handy. As the boat listed, he made an effort and, swimming alongside, caught the guard of the boat with one hand. One of the men aboard grasped him by the wrist and in a moment, he was pulled on deck, a little shook up, but none the worse for his perilous adventure. It was a close call.

Dec. 25, 1886 WA

Thos. S. Brian, nightwatchman on the *Ordway*, was drowned in the Willamette at Portland on last Saturday evening, while landing at Weidler's mill. His brother, Mike, was drowned off the O.R. & N. dock here about two years ago. The body of the man drowned last Saturday was recovered yesterday evening.

Dec. 25, 1886 WA

Last Thursday evening, Chas. Johnson, fishing for the Anglo-American Packing Co., started above Tongue Point to put out his net. A squall coming up, he told the boat puller to take down the sail. While doing so, the boom flew around and hit Johnson, knocking him overboard, and throwing the boatpuller between it and the gunwale of the boat. Before he could recover himself, his unfortunate companion had disappeared. The drowned man was a Russian Finn, unmarried, 28 years of age. His countrymen offer $25 reward for the recovery of the body.

April 23, 1887 DA

Two Drowned; One Missing

The sad sight of drowned bodies borne to the undertaker's to be prepared for decent sepulture, was again seen yesterday afternoon, two poor fellows whose troubles on earth are over, being arrayed in the habiliments of the grave.

The first was the body of Gus. Mattson, a Russian Finn, aged 24, fishing in boat *No. 12* of the Cutting Packing Co., who with his boat puller was drowned off Clatsop spit Friday morning. The body was found by A. K. Weir Friday evening, where it had washed ashore on Clatsop beach near the wreck of the *Cairnsmuir*. The body was wrapped in the net, and the boat, oars, etc., had also come ashore a short distance from the body; the watch in the pocket of the drowned man had stopped at twenty-five minutes past five. It appeared as though he had tried to beach his boat, but unsuccessfully. The boat puller is missing; and was in all probability drowned also; no tidings has yet been received of his body. Deceased was well spoken of as a hard working young man who saved his money and was trying to get on and get a start in the world. He had $26.35 in his pocket, and is said to have had a handsome sum at interest in one of the banks. He was a member of the Columbia river fishermen's protective union, and will be buried by that association at ten o'clock this morning.

The name of the missing boat puller could not be ascertained. Later in the afternoon, G. Compare, fishing Geo. W. Hume's boat *No. 9*, brought up the body of a drowned man that he had found floating at Scarborough head. It had been in the water for some time and was so decomposed as to be unrecognizable.

May 21, 1887 DA

THE LIFE SAVING STATION.

Major Blakeney and Prof. Von Beyer have selected a site for the location of the Point Adams life saving station, subject to the approval of the secretary of the treasury. The spot determined upon is in the cove to the eastward of fort Stevens, at a point about the middle of the donation claim of B.C. Kindred.

It is proposed to provide the new station with a new life boat of greater capacity than any now in the service, as well as a self-righting and self-bailing surf boat. The station will be furnished with the most improved appliances of the life saving service, and will be manned with a trained crew. There will be some necessary delay in commencing the work, but Major Blakeney hopes that representations to the proper authorities will enable a life saving crew to be established at that point in time to render services to unfortunate fishermen or others next season. In the ordinary course of such matters, if everything goes well, the station would probably be ready for efficient service some time about next fall. When the safety of so many lives is concerned, the establishment can be made none too soon, and Major Blakeney and Prof. Von Beyer deserve credit for their endeavors to expedite the location of a life saving crew at the Point Adams station.

Nov. 26, 1887 WA

One of Cook's fishermen in his boat yesterday morning near Clifton, while about to shoot a sea lion, accidentally shot himself in the right thigh, the ball shattering the bone. He was brought down to the hospital and given surgical aid.

May 3, 1888 AB

A short time ago August Tano and John Heikkila, two young men recently arrived here, bought a net and rented a boat, number five, from the Columbia River Packing company and last Monday started to fish, since which time nothing has been heard of them til yesterday afternoon when one of the cannery boats reports finding near fort Stevens a fragment of the net they had bought. It is feared that both the men have perished.

May 27, 1888 DA

A report from below is to the effect that on the 24th inst, Booth's boat *No. 20* went into a fish trap at Baker's bay, and that the captain, Abram Kemila, and his boat puller, were both drowned. The boat puller whose name could not be ascertained, leaves a wife and two children in Humboldt, Cal. The boat and net were recovered.

May 29, 1888 DA

Mishaps on the river, though not as numerous as in some former years, are still sadly frequent. Henry Matson, whose death outside the bar was previously announced, leaves a wife and three children in Uniontown; nothing has yet been heard further from August Tano and John Heikkila, who are now missing for over a week. The body of Jno. Waydie, who was drowned at Clifton last Saturday evening, was given interment yesterday.

May 29, 1888 DA

The body of an unknown drowned man came ashore at Sand island yesterday. Acting coroner Surprenant will go down this morning to see if the remains can be identified.

June 5, 1888 DA

Drowned Last Evening

A distressing accident took place at upper Astoria last evening by which a man named Daniel Sullivan lost his life. He was employed on the steamer *A.B. Field*, now lying at Leinenweber's dock. In some way he slipped and fell into the water, although in ten minutes from the time he fell into the water, the body was recovered and medical aid secured, life was found to be extinct and all efforts to resuscitate him were useless. While in India some years ago, Sullivan received a severe sunstroke and ever since was subject to fainting spells. It is supposed that in this way he lost consciousness and upon striking the water was unable to exert himself or keep afloat, and so drowned.

June 7, 1888 DA

Last Tuesday evening Della Gore, the young daughter of C.E. Gore, engineer on the Northern Pacific transfer boat *Tacoma*, was drowned at Hunter's Point. She was walking along the shore, and stepping on a spot where the water had washed out the bank, her footing gave away and she fell into the river. An hour later the body was recovered.

June 7, 1888 DA

The body found on Sand island a few days ago has been identified as that of Abraham Kemila, who was drowned in Baker's bay from one of Booth's fishing boats on the afternoon of May 25th. The funeral will be from F.H.

Surprenant & Co.'s undertaking rooms at half-past nine this morning, under the auspices of the Columbia River Fishermen's Protective Union.

June 8, 1888 DA

The body of a man with part of the left hand gone was picked up near Knappton yesterday and brought to the coroner here for identification. It is found to be the body of Jacob Brenell [Rinell], which was lost from the *Gleaner* off Tongue Point, last January.

June 11, 1888 DA

Five fishermen were picked up in the outside breakers by the life crew at Cape Hancock last Tuesday morning; one of the tugs is reported to have picked up five more. A large net was found on the weather beach yesterday morning, this side of Tinkers. No loss of life has been reported.

June 11, 1888 DA

Geo. T. Myers' boat *No. 29* capsized off point Ellice yesterday, the men and net were saved, the boat drifted off and is probably lost.

June 15, 1888 DA

Drowned Fisherman Found.

EDITOR ASTORIAN:

On Chinook beach, June 11th, found a drowned fisherman; dark complexion, about 5 feet 6 inches in height; about 30 years of age; had been in the water about three weeks. Nothing but a roll of ladies twist tobacco in his pocket; his clothing consisted of blue undershirt, cotton checkered shirt; over that, knitted jersey overshirt, blue cotton jumper and pants; blue flannel drawers; No. 8 gum boots. He was put in a home-made coffin and buried in the grave inside of highest tidewater mark. He wore a piece of leadline around the loins for a belt. Further information may be had as to whereabouts of the grave, etc., of

REES WILLIAMS, Justice of the Peace.
Chinook Beach, June 12, 1888.

June 15, 1888 DA

NEWS FROM ILWACO.

Drowning of John Johansen.—Stormy Weather At The Cape.

EDITOR ASTORIAN:

A fisherman who was caught in the severe gale Wednesday night had his boat so badly damaged that he was compelled to cast his net overboard to keep the boat afloat; to prevent the net being lost, he tied it to a trap in Baker's Bay; yesterday morning, he, with some other fishermen, went out to get the net; in hauling it in they found entangled another net, and in this net the body of a man, who proved to be John Johansen, a native of Sweden, who has been fishing for the Occident cannery this season; his boat was found bottom side up farther up the bay. When found, he had on but pants and undershirt, having evidently taken off his rubber boots and coat before the boat overturned, the better to battle with the angry waves; he was known to be a powerful swimmer—having saved a man from drowning in San Francisco bay, last year; when his boat capsized, he is supposed to have become entangled in the net, and thus rendered powerless, carried to his untimely end. Nothing has been heard of his boat puller but it is more than likely he also has been drowned. He, Johansen, fished on the Columbia last summer and for the past two winters has been running out from Frisco in coasters. He was about 26 years of age and has no relatives in this country. The secretary of the Sailors' Union in San Francisco will most likely know the address of his parents.

The severe storm for the past four days has caused a great deal of trouble to the railroad company in breaking the booms of piles and preventing the diver from working.

Joe Surprenant has the honor of being the first bather of the season; in securing some piling the other night, his boat was overturned and Joe's manly form was plunged into the angry waters, but aside from a cold bath no damage was done.

Some of the trapmen have not been able to lift their traps for three days on account of the heavy winds. June 16, 1888 DA

DROWNED FROM THEIR BOATS
Sad Tidings From the Mouth of the River.

Since Wednesday, there has been rough weather at the mouth of the river, and there have been several accidents among the fishing fleet. When the *Gen. Canby* arrived at 2:30 yesterday afternoon, she had on board the dead body of John Johansen, of boat *No. 18*, Occident Packing company, who was drowned in Baker's bay night before last. It was also reported that Harry Hendrickson of Elmore & Sanborn's boat No. 18, was drowned yesterday morning, and that three of the boats of the Astoria Packing Co. had capsized, the occupants being rescued. The wind was blowing so strong when the *Canby* left the cape yesterday that none of the boats in the bay dare venture out. The identity of the body described in yesterday's ASTORIAN has not yet been learned.

LATER.—The steamer *Electric* arrived in later, and reports trying to get a boat belonging to the Astoria Packing co. that is bottom up on Desdemona sands. The boat could get within 25 yards of the capsized boat, but the breakers were too rough to justify closer approach.

When six boats were off Flavel's Tansy point wharf yesterday morning, four of them were capsized. The occupants were all able to scramble up on the bottoms of the submerged boats from which they were afterwards rescued, except one man in Astoria Packing Co.'s boat *No. 17*, named John Frederickson, who was drowned. He was aged 23 years and leaves a mother and two sisters.

This makes four reported drowned and it is thought the sad list will be increased two or three more, as a number of boats are still missing.

LATER. Reports from below say that Harry Frederickson is not drowned; he sends word from Sand Island to Fort Stevens that his net is fouled and he is cleaning it.

The following additional report is handed in.

A boat from Kinney while sailing to town this morning capsized below Smith's point in the channel. The captain, T. Toeikala, was saved, and the boat puller Jakob Nilkula, a native of Finland, aged 38, was drowned.

61

Capt. McVicar of the tug Donald, while coming up from below, picked up three capsized boats and crews.

Experienced fishermen say it was one of the suddenest and severest squalls they ever experienced. With the exception of John Johanson, who was drowned in Baker's Bay, it does not seem that any foresight, or care could have prevented the terrible series of fatal accidents near the mouth of the river during the past two or three days.

June 16, 1888 DA

Harry Hendrickson, who was reported drowned, turned up all right yesterday. He says that he would have stayed down where he was engaged in clearing his net, but hearing the report he was drowned, came up to town.

June 17, 1888 DA

When Gus. Benjus, fishing for Astoria Packing Co., went down yesterday morning to get his boat, it was gone, but out in the stream hitched to the spar buoy was a boat that looked like his. Going out it was found to be his boat which some thieves had stolen during the night and taking it out to the spar buoy, took the sail, mast, stunsail and net and decamped with the plunder.

June 17, 1888 DA

Gus Snugg, fishing for M.J. Kinney, is not in very good luck of late. Last Friday his boat was capsized by a squall, and he narrowly escaped drowning. Yesterday he was putting out in the stream just as the incoming *Oregonian* was going by, and was again capsized by the steamer. He and his boat puller were rescued, the boat was damaged some and the net was lost.

June 19, 1888 DA

The body of an unknown man was found Saturday on the beach near McKinzie's point. The coroner from Ilwaco precinct held an inquest, and the remains, which were in an advanced stage of decomposition, were buried near the place where found. Deceased was about 38 years old, sandy complexion, and about 5 feet 10 inches in height, wore a brown suit and kip leather boots, was evidently a fisherman, but nothing could be found to identify him.

June 19, 1888 DA

Two dead bodies found on Sand Island yesterday, sad memories of last week's stormy weather. Thus far they have not been identified, but an effort will be made in that direction to-day.

June 20, 1888 DA

The dead body reported in yesterday's ASTORIAN as having been found at McKenzie's head last Saturday, and given temporary burial proves to be the remains of Henry Mattson, who was drowned outside the bar in his fishing boat on the 23rd of last month. The remains will be disinterred, and will be brought over for burial tomorrow.

June 20, 1888 DA

A SAD DEATH LIST.

The following is furnished by the secretary of the Columbia River Fishermen's Protective Union, and is a corrected list of the fishermen drowned in the Columbia river from May 1st to June 19th, 1888:

John Hekkila, native of Finland, fishing for Sam'l Elmore, drowned May 10th; August Tano, native of Finland, fishing for Sam'l Elmore, drowned May 10th, Abram Kummela, native of Finland, fishing for A. Booth, drowned May 17th (body recovered); Henry Mattson, native of Finland, fishing for Sam'l Elmore, drowned May 21 (body recovered); John Wayde, native of Finland, fishing for J.W. & V. Cook, drowned May 27th (body recovered); Albert Hiltula, native of Finland, fishing for A. Booth, drowned May 27th; Gus Shuit, native of Germany, fishing for Sam'l Elmore, drowned May 27th; Mat Mattson, native of Finland, fishing for Occident Packing Co., drowned June 15; Olof Johnson, native of Finland, fishing for Occident Packing Co. drowned June 15th (body recovered); J. Hendrickson, native of Finland, fishing for Astoria Pkg. Co. drowned June 16th; Frank Fletcher, native of Scotland, fishing for J.W. & V. Cook, drowned June 16th; Chas. Gustinson, and boat puller (name unknown), fishing for Astoria Packing co., drowned June 18th.

June 30, 1888 DMA

The dead body found on the beach between the slaughter [house] and the buoy depot last Sunday proves to be the remains of Theodore Sitgass, who was drowned in the Columbia above Tongue Point, about two months ago. Some keys that he had in his pocket which fitted his trunk, and a match safe that Wm. Bock gave him while hunting together, served to identify him. Deceased was a native of Mecklenburg, Germany, and was in the 38th year of his age. He leaves a brother living near Portland. The funeral will be this morning at Clatsop.

June 30, 1888 DMA

Accidental Drowning

Last Sunday evening, the steamer *Tonquin* was passing Jno. A. Devlin's cannery, and was about to tie up to the dock. Jno. Carter, a deck hand, went aft to throw out a line, Not hearing the usual response, the captain followed to see what was the matter and saw Carter struggling in the water astern. He flung him a rope, which the unfortunate man failed to hold; again the captain dropped a line directly on his arms, but he appeared paralyzed and sank without an effort. He was a Canadian, aged 32 years, and a stranger here, not having been on the boat a week. The body has not been recovered.

Oct. 20, 1888 DA

A later article, not printed here, suggests that that the captain murdered the Canadian.

Yesterday morning between one and two o'clock, P. Bocasowitch, of fishing boat *No. 39* belonging to Geo. Hume, was returning from down towards the bar and, dropping his boat around to the net racks on the roadway, was sur-

SAVED FROM DEATH
Narrow Escape of a Man from Drowning

prised to hear faint groans proceeding from underneath. After some investigation, he found a man in the last stages of exhaustion in the water under the net racks, sticking in the mud and ooze up to his knees and unable to speak or stir or do more than feebly moan. He was livid with cold.

Boscowitch secured assistance and the man, whose name could not be learned, was removed to a place of shelter, and his life saved.

April 6, 1889 DA

Narrow Escape for McLaren

Jno. McLaren had an experience last night that will make him wonder when he reads this item that he is still in the land of the living.

Last night, while a little howcomeyouso, he fell from the Main [9th] street wharf into the dark and rapidly flowing Columbia. When he came to the surface, he yelled. Albert Byer and Jas. Burchall, of the steamer *Alliance* heard him. They saw McLaren, skillfully flung him a line and pulled him to safety. He owes those two ready men a vote of thanks. Had it not been for them, the tom cod and porgies would now be nibbling at his ears at the bottom of the river.

After reviving, McLaren showed up at THE ASTORIAN office; the rain was falling heavily; "where's your hat?" asked the reporter. "At the bottom of the river; this doesn't often happen," said McLaren.

Then A.W. Utzinger came along and took him to his home where he boards, at Mrs. Daggett's. *August 27, 1889 DA*

A DEPLORABLE ACCIDENT

James Thompson, a well known resident of this city, was drowned from off the steamer *R.R. Thompson*, this side of Westport, at 2:40 yesterday afternoon. The steamer had left Westport on her way down, and was near the mouth of the slough. Thompson was last seen on the lower deck, and was not seen to fall in the water. Suddenly Messrs. Smith, Anstinsen, and other Astoria passengers saw him as he rose to the surface, astern of the boat. The boat was immediately stopped; a small boat lowered, but when within about a hundred feet of the unfortunate man, who was making desperate efforts to reach the boat, he sank, and was seen no more.

Deceased was a steady and exemplary young man, about 29 years of age, and came to this city from Vincennes, Indiana. He was a nephew of Mrs. Badollett. He had but recently returned from Alaska, where he was a stockholder in the Chilcat Canning Co., where he had spent last summer.

He was a member of Pacific Lodge No. 17, K. of P., of this city. A delegation from the lodge chartered the steamer *Electric* last evening and left at nine o'clock to make an effort to recover the body.

Nov. 17, 1889 DA

64

COLUMBIA RIVER FISHING FLEET, ASTORIA, ORE.

W. WHITMAN,
ASTORIA, ORE.

N○ 4.

Salmon Canning, Astoria, Oregon.

5222. STURGEON ON THE COLUMBIA RIVER, OREGON.

COPYRIGHT, 1899, BY DETROIT PHOTOGRAPHIC CO.

STEELHEADS
10 & 11.LBS
BLUEBACKS
6 LBS
COPYRIGHTED
BY
J. H. BRATT.
1895.

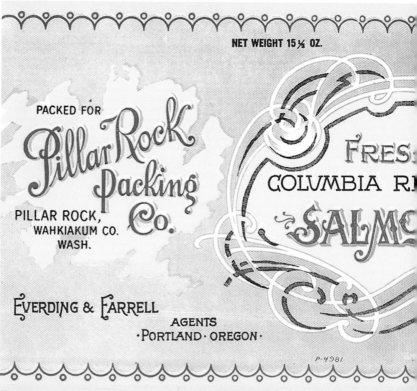

EPICURE

TRADE  MARK

REGISTERED

BRAND

SCHMIDT L & LITH. CO. S.F.

·PILLAR· ·ROCK· BRAND

·COLUMBIA· ·RIVER·

SPRING PACK

Mammoth Sturgeon Caught at Astoria.

Columbia River Salmon Boat.

Oyster boats used in Willapa Bay just north of Columbia River.

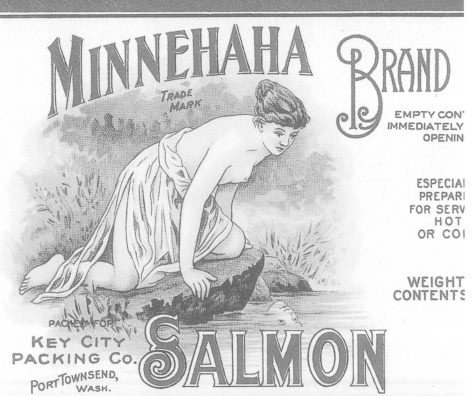

THE 1890'S

A TEMPERANCE LECTURE.

Last Friday morning Wm. Gulk, a young man aged 29 years, started from here to go to work on Young's river. He had been working on the Walluski. At the old mill site he got a boat and pulled up Young's river. Elmer Warnstaff, who is running a scow from the pulp mill, saw and hailed him, but he paid no attention; he was intoxicated at the time. That was the last seen of him alive.

About 6 o'clock yesterday afternoon, a human arm was seen projecting above the surface of the water on a mud flat opposite the old mill. Investigation brought to the surface the body of the missing Gulk.

The remains will be brought to the morgue this morning. Under the circumstances it is thought unnecessary to hold an inquest.

March 7, 1890 DA

Last evening just before dark a man and woman started to cross the river in a small boat, intending to go over to Knappton, six miles distant. The man was very much intoxicated and the woman but little better off. They would evidently have been swept away by the tide, and the bystanders realizing this fact, some men went out in a boat, brought back the inebriates and they were taken away to sleep off the effects of the liquor.

April 13, 1890 DA

Yesterday morning a man in an intoxicated condition came up to Carnahan's ship in a skiff in which were eight salmon. On attempting to land he capsized the skiff, thus throwing the salmon into the bay. After floundering around for a while the man managed to secure three of the fish, the other five floating out to sea. It was fun for the boys to see the man trying to get his fish while in an intoxicated condition.

April 15, 1890 DA

Drowned at the Clatsop Mill

John Duncan, a young man of 25, recently from Colorado, met his death at the Clatsop mill last Sunday afternoon. He, in company with others, was moving lumber and as one piece came out of the chute he jumped to escape being hit by it. He fell overboard, and did not rise to the surface. The body was rescued later in the afternoon. The funeral will be at eight o'clock this morning.

April 15, 1890 DA

This morning at eight o'clock, the funeral of John Duncan will take place, and the Clatsop mill will shut down in order that the employes may attend. He was drowned on Sunday, as described in THE ASTORIAN yesterday morning, and the funeral was announced to take place yesterday, but was postponed until today.

April 16, 1890 DA

DROWNING OF ERIC JACOBS

Chinook, Wash., April 11, 1891

An accident occurred here this morning that resulted in the drowning of Eric Jacobs, one of our boatmen here. Early this morning he and another man by the name of Manderson took a boat and started from the cannery wharf to go to Chinook river after another boat. Soon after starting out they ran against a pile, and the shock combined with the force of the current upset the boat and threw the two men out. Manderson kicked off his boots and swam and drifted about a mile and a half, when he was picked up by men in another boat. Jacobs disappeared almost immediately after the boat upset and was at once drowned. The body was recovered yesterday afternoon.

April 12, 1891 DMA

For some time past, Major Blakeney, superintendent of the lifesaving service for the twelth district, has endeavored to obtain a large lifeboat for service on the coast. He has now succeeded in obtaining the permission of the general superintendent, and tenders for building the boat on the Pacific coast are now called for.

The boat is to be a self-righting, self-bailing craft, with water ballast and center board. In length, she will be 34 feet, 8 feet beam, 3 feet 6 inches amidships and 6 feet deep at the stem and stern. In the construction of the boat, the keel, bilge, keelson, stem, stern, aft and forward deadwood are to be of the best white oak. The floors are to be of hackmetack and the outside planking of two layers of clear Honduras mahogany is to be laid on the frames diagonally. The centerboard is to be of gun metal, 8 feet 8 inches long, 25 inches wide and 1 inch thick. Bulkheads and centerboard trunk are to be constructed of yellow pine.

In all available spaces between the deck and top of keelsons, copper air cases are to be fitted, and in order to enable the boat to free herself of water, relieving valves of the most approved pattern are provided. Every piece of iron to be used in building the boat is to be forged, and no fastenings other than copper or gun metal are to be allowed.

Two masts 18 and 16 feet long, with sprit sails and jib, will form the rig. The craft will carry a crew of eight men.

This type of boat has been found eminently suited for the arduous work on the English coast. Capsized in a heavy sea, the boat will right herself in a few moments, and no matter how much water she takes on board, the ejecting apparatus speedily frees her.

May 3, 1891 DA

Sand island is not as populous as it has been in former years. The days of fishing on and outside the bar are gone. The jetty has so increased the flow of the current that, practically, there is no flood; it is all ebb, and boats cannot stem the rushing water.

May 14, 1891 DMA

A plunger swamped at Chinook beach last Friday afternoon and its five occupants were in peril in rough water. Twice a boat was launched from the shore, each time being overturned. A third time proved successful, and all five were rescued from drowning, none too soon, as they were exhausted from their struggles to keep afloat.

June 7, 1891 DA

Over fourteen hundred boats have their headquarters at Astoria. Hundreds of thousands of dollars are annually paid out here for tin-plate, twine, salt and cannery supplies.

June 20, 1891 DMA

A zephyr from the south ruffled the blue waters of the bay yesterday, and one of the fishing boats was upset, with no damage to the occupants beyond a wetting.

June 20, 1891 DMA

"My papa has only caught seven fish in three nights," said a little 6-year-old girl on the roadway yesterday, "and he does be so tired when he comes home."

June 27, 1891 DMA

Up to Sunday morning it was the subject of congratulations that there were so few fatalities on the river among the fishermen this season, but during the closing hours of the salmon season of '91, three unfortunate men lost their lives.

The steamer *Mexico*, from Alaska, crossed in last Sunday night from Alaska, when off Tanzy point she ran into one of A. Booth & Co.'s boats; the unfortunate occupants were asleep, and woke only to see the huge iron hull of the steamship as it bore down over them. They rose after the vessel passed, and shouted for help. The steamer came to anchor, two boats were put out, and search was made for a long time, but to no purpose; they were drowned. A part of the net was found wrapped around the propeller. There was another boat lying close by, the occupants of which were also asleep.

It is said that the boat carried no lights and in the darkness it was impossible for those on the *Mexico* to see the boat. The *Mexico* started up at day break and docked at the U.P. wharf. The boat was picked up toward the bar in a battered condition yesterday afternoon.

The steamer *T.J. Potter* when on the way up from here last Sunday night ran into a fishing boat near Cathlamet and one of the occupants was drowned. The *Potter* upon striking the boat stopped, put off a search boat and rescued one of the men. The names of none of the three could be ascertained.

August 11, 1891 DA

A DREADFUL ACCIDENT.

One of those dreadful occurrences which shock an entire community, took place in the upper part of town yesterday evening, resulting in the death of little Hazel Hanthorn, aged 6, daughter of Mr. and Mrs. J.O. Hanthorn, and Charles Strom, a well known resident of the city.

About 6 o'clock yesterday evening, Mr. Strom was engaged in building a boat in the cannery formerly occupied by W.D. Smith, and little Hazel, the pet and pride of the household was playing around the premises. There were holes in the floor and through one of these traps the poor little thing dropped into the cold dark water beneath.

With a heroism that commands itself to all who admire valor, the man sprang after the child, to rescue her, but only fell to his death. In falling, he must have struck something and become stunned. Just what did happen can not be clearly stated, for unfortunately, the only witness of the accident was a man who could speak no English, and it was a painfully long time, and precious minutes elapsed before he was able to secure assistance or make known the tragedy that was taking place underneath the building.

It was nearly half an hour before assistance arrived. When found, the little girl was on the man's shoulders, her little hands clasped around him in the rigidity of death. Life was evidently extinct in both bodies, and despite the most strenuous efforts on the part of the physicians summoned, it was evident that all attempts at resuscitation were useless.

The grief of the stricken mother of the sunny haired darling and of the wife of the brave man who met his death in an effort to rescue the child was a sight to move the coldest hearted to tears.

Mr. Hanthorn, who was in Portland, was immediately wired, and will be here on the *Thompson* this morning.

Chas. Strom was a man about 40 years of age, and highly respected by his associates. He was a member of Seaside Lodge A.O.U.W., Astor Lodge K. of P. and Beaver Lodge I.O.O.F.

Sept. 9, 1891 DMA

While bailing out a scow at Jim Crow Sands, one of Enyart's workmen forgot to replace the plug before relaunching the scow and thus narrowly escaped death. The night was stormy, and about 8 o'clock one of the men discovered that the scow was sinking. Those on board climbed on the roof for safety and left some horses which were on board to their fate. The sides of the shanty were broken by the force of the waves and one of the horses swept overboard. The animal managed to get its forefeet on the edge of the scow and remained in that position the entire night. The damage done was slight.

October 18, 1891 DA

A FATAL ACCIDENT
Drowned in the Bay Yesterday Morning

Charles Nelson, bargemaster on barge *No. 7*, was drowned in Scow bay between 7 and 8 o'clock yesterday morning. The steamer *Cascades* arrived down with three barges in tow, which were anchored as usual. When the steamer passed the barges everything was all right but when the *Geo. H. Mendell* shortly after went up to hook on and take the barges to Ft. Stevens, Nelson was missing.

He had got out a bucket and began swabbing the deck as soon as the barge was anchored, and then coiled some lines, and it is supposed that a sudden lurch of the barge sent him over. He could not swim a stroke, and thus was drowned.

Men were dragging for the body all day but to no avail. He was a single man, a native of Sweden, aged 36 years, and leaves a mother in the old country.

October 31, 1891 DA

DROWNED FROM HIS BOAT

Last Monday evening Coroner Surprenant was visited by a young man named Elliott, from Elliott's landing, who told him that he had just come down from Brownsville (about fifteen miles up the river on the Oregon side), where he had found the dead body of a man lying near a boat.

The coroner chartered the steamer *Improvement*, and at 1 o'clock yesterday morning, after a pleasant five hours in the storm, he finally found the place on the river shore where the dead man had been brought. He was brought down here yesterday morning. Young Elliott was the only one who had any definite information. The man's name was L.W. Hunt; he was a native of Bangor, Me.; he had been fishing for William Hume at Eagle Cliff, for the last six years. His boat and net are now there. Since the fishing season closed, he has been living in a house near Knappa with a man named Sawyer. Last Saturday, he started in a very small flat-bottomed skiff to go across to an island to hunt ducks. That was the last seen of him alive. When found, the body was in the water under the boat; the boat had lodged between two logs that came together, diagonally. He had started to take off one boot, and socks and the strings of his decoy ducks were wound around his legs. He had evidently fallen overboard Saturday night and perished miserably in the darkness.

Coroner Surprenant received a telegram from Mr. Hume yesterday afternoon, requesting that a decent burial be given the body.

It was deemed unnecessary to hold an inquest. The funeral will be at Greenwood cemetery to-morrow.

Nov. 4, 1891 DMA

Jeff Gentry is trying hard to economize these hard times. He was working at the Fishermen's Packing Co. putting in a new foundation when he made up his mind he would save 25 cents, the price of a bath, by falling overboard, which he forthwith proceeded to do. His friends fished him out and laid him on the sunny side of the building. Jeff says he likes water on the side.

Apr. 7, 1893 ADB

About 2 o'clock Sunday morning, a man in an intoxicated condition fell off the Main street dock alongside the steamer *Manzanita*. He was rescued by the watchman and one of the crew of the steamer, in a badly demoralized condition.

Apr. 10, 1893 ADB

A PERILOUS POSITION
Floating Down the Lewis and Clarke on a Capsized Boat.

J. R. Mathers, wife and son, met with an accident yesterday, which might have ended disastrously to all of them had it not been for the timely assistance of Billy Larsen, the milkman.

Accompanied by his wife and son, Mr. Mathers started in a large fish boat yesterday from Knappa for his homestead on the Lewis and Clark for the purpose of putting his farm in operation, pruning his fruit trees, etc. The wind was quite puffy all the way, but when they reached the Lewis and Clarke, a sudden squall caused some of the lines to come loose from the boom and the next puff capsized the boat, sending her over on her side where she rested on the sail which was lying flat on the water. Away they sailed with the tide, holding on to their seats like grim death, and yelling to attract the attention of some of the people along the banks. They had floated around about an hour when Billy Larsen spied them, and he lost no time getting a boat out to them and saving them from watery graves. He then took them to his residence, supplied them with dry clothing and provided them with every comfort, for which they feel more than thankful to Billy and his estimable wife. The accident was a great misfortune to the family, as they are working people and are not blessed with an abundance of this world's goods. All of Mrs. Mather's clothing was lost, as was all the supplies that they were taking to the farm.

Apr. 11, 1893 ADB

HE WAS DESERTED.
Jens Nielson Has Something to Say.

The following item appeared in the BUDGET yesterday, and the statement from Mr. Nielson explains matters more satisfactorily:

Jens Nielsen and his boat puller, fishing for George & Barker's cannery, came very near getting drowned yesterday. When off Chinook point, their boat was capsized in a squall. They succeeded in getting back on top of the boat and were being rapidly carried down the river when a boat put out from shore and rescued them from their perilous position. The boat and net were lost as it was too stormy to try and save them.

Astoria, April 22, 1893
EDITOR BUDGET:

On the 20 inst., in the morning between 6 and 9 o'clock, I left Hungry Harbor or Megler's station where I had been lying from 11 a.m. on the day previous, with many other boats. Some were there when I came and others came afterwards. As everybody started, I thought I would also, as there were several boats together in case of an accident, we could assist one another, but such was not the case. I lifted anchor and pulled out, and before I reached the point, a puff of wind struck the boat and filled her and turned her bottom up. We managed to get on top and saw two boats, one about fifty and the other 100 yards off. I supposed we would be picked up, as I saw the men in the other boats looking at us, and we shouted for them to come; but no, they did not, but sailed off and left us to the mercy of the seas. As I came home at 9 o'clock, the same evening, one man by the name of Emil Ericson, fishing for George & Barker reported having seen the boat turn over and the two men on the bottom, but did not attempt to save them. Another man by the name of Jackson, who I am told was Christ Jackson, also reported seeing us. Fred Bang stated this to Mary G. Haven. She asked him if the men were saved. The answer was no, as long as they could see them, they were on the bottom of the boat going down with a strong ebb tide. I would like to know how such heartless men would feel under such circumstances, sitting on a boat in a heavy sea with water constantly breaking over them, and nobody making any effort to save them? What are such men worth? Have they any feelings for suffering humanity?

I took up my watch to see what time it was; and it was then 20 minutes past 8 o'clock. We drifted down toward Mr. McGowans, being way out in the channel. I stood up and waved my hat, hoping someone might see us as that was the last chance. As good luck had it, the men were out bailing out their boats and they happened to see us. As all the boats were swamped, they got hold of a big trap skiff, which Christ Hauge, Louis Hauffe, R. Pederson and P. Holstein managed to get out to us and took us off and landed us behind Scarborough hill. The men took us up to old man Fannings at 10 o'clock, where we were furnished with dry clothing, where we got warmed up, and when we were able to walk, we went down to McGowan's where we were treated kindly until we left on the steamer *Queetrin* the evening and were landed in Astoria about 8:45 in the evening.

I wish to extend my heartfelt thanks to those good men who had the courage and manliness to save us, and also to those kind people who treated us so well.
    JENS NIELSON

Mr. Nielson stated that the boat and net was on Chinook beach, and in all probability pretty badly broken up as they ran through one fish trap and broke out twenty-one of the piling and another one and broke out six.
April 22, 1893 ADB

Yesterday afternoon, as Charley, the son of C.W. Stone, was riding a bicycle on Flavel's dock, and when near the slip on Cass [10th] street, the machine struck a taut rope, throwing the boy headlong overboard into the river. As the boy could swim a little, he managed to keep on top until rescued by the aid of a rope, none the worse for his involuntary ducking.
Apr. 24, 1893 ADB

THE PERILS OF THE DEEP
Four Fishermen Drowned Yesterday

At 4 o'clock yesterday afternoon, 900 fish boats from different canneries on the river had their nets out off Sand island. A few minutes after and without warning, a storm burst over the river, accompanied by a terrible wind and high sea. Some 200 boats managed to get under the lea shore of Sand island and saved themselves. The balance, unable from their position to beat around, made for home. The storm was now at its worst, and two boats from Kinney's cannery and one from the Cutting Packing company were capsized, throwing out the occupants and burying the sails of the boats under the waves. The little steamer *Occident*, which happened to be near, went to the rescue of the men and luckily saved them, although the boats were allowed to drift to sea. A few minutes after, in plain sight of the docks along the water front, another boat turned bottom up. The next moment two more capsized about 100 feet away from her, and though over thirty of the fishing fleet were sailing around them, no help could be extended to the unfortunate ones. The steamer *Electric* went to the rescue and picked up four men out of the six, the two that were lost being Nels Hanson and George Raith, fishing for the Cutting Packing company. The rescued men state that both men sank out of sight, calling for assistance. Meanwhile the fury of the storm was playing havoc with the sails of the boats tearing them to ribbons. The steamer *Wenona*, Capt. Job Lamly, on the way from Knappton, saw a boat capsize and at once made for her, but before the steamer reached her, boat, net, sails and occupants had disappeared. The boat also belonged to the Cutting Packing company. The names of the unfortunate men could not be learned. There is no doubt but they have perished. The balance of the fleet got safely to the canneries.

May 12, 1893 ADB

Yesterday afternoon about 4 o'clock, H.O. Hendrickson and his boat puller, Victor Aleene, were fishing on Clatsop spit, close to the jetty, with boat *No. 133* of Kinney's cannery, when without a moment's warning a tremendous breaker broke over them, capsizing the boat and throwing the men out. Hendrickson managed to climb on the upturned boat, but Aleene was sucked under by the breakers and before help could be rendered, the unfortunate man drowned and his body was carried out to sea. Hendrickson was rescued by the occupants of another boat which was lying near by. The boat and net were also saved, the rigging and gear lost. Aleene was a single man, a native of Finland, aged about 31 years. He leaves two sisters in Portland and one in San Francisco. One of his sisters now living in Portland is the wife of Wm. Anderson, until lately living in this city. The deceased was a member of the C.R.F.P.U.

Columbia River Fishermen's Protective Union
May 24, 1893 ADB

The captain of the life-saving crew at Cape Hancock is very much dissatisfied with the boat in which their duties so often compel them to embark on stormy waters. Unlike the boat used by the crew at Point Adams, it is not a self-righter and has to be bailed out by hand. In addition to this disadvantage, it is not considered staunch enough for the rough seas with which it has to contend.

May 26, 1893 ADB

STRUCK BY THE BREAKERS.

Mr. Ole B. Olsen, one of the sufferers in yesterday's accident to a fishing boat near Sand Island, called at the office to-day with an introductory note from our esteemed friend, Mr. Sofus Jensen, secretary of the Fishermen's union, and kindly gave us an account of the affair. About 2 o'clock yesterday, he and his partner, Anton Sumstad, who own their own boat and fish for the Point Adams

Packing company, were lying with their boat just below the old wreck of the *Great Republic*, their net out. It was not very rough at the time and they apprehended no danger, when suddenly a great breaker loomed up with a menacing crest close upon them. There was no time to get the boat bow on and in another moment the rushing avalanche of water struck them. Both of the men were hurled from the boat, Olsen much further away than his companion, who soon regained the boat and held on. Olsen saw his only chance and swam to the net. He soon gathered together a number of the net's buoys, which kept him afloat, but his sufferings were intense and his peril supreme, as the breakers repeatedly swept over and submerged him, so that he was completely exhausted and more than half dead when both of them were gallantly rescued by the life-saving crew from Cape Hancock. Then the captain and crew of the life boat stripped the nearly inanimate form of Olsen and gave him a vigorous rubbing. When he had sufficiently recovered, they clothed him with contributions from their own stores. The imperiled fishermen are loud in their praise of the life crew for the noble treatment they received at the scene of the accident and on shore. James Nelson also did a generous act for them. He was fishing below them and went to the rescue, losing part of his own net to save theirs.

May 26, 1893 ADB

Yesterday morning, the body of Ole Straud, who was fishing for George & Barker, was picked up at Sand Island by Richard Welcome and brought to this city and turned over to Coroner Pohl. Straud was fishing in boat No. 14 and on Tuesday, May 16th during the heavy blow, capsized. The boat puller, whose name could not be learned, was also drowned. The deceased was aged 29 years, a native of Norway, and has an uncle who is fishing somewhere on the river.

May 31, 1893 ADB

Word was received from Seaside this morning that the body of a man had been picked up on the beach near there. Coroner Pohl will send over some person to bring up the body.

June 1, 1893 ADB

Deputy Coroner R M Stuart returned from Clatsop this morning where he had been to view the body that was picked up there yesterday. It was so badly decomposed that it was utterly impossible to recognize the features. The body was buried where found.

June 2, 1893 ADB

During slack water, the only time when fishing is possible near the mouth of the river, there is always a boat from the Canby life-saving station lying off the south side of Peacock spit, all manned and ready to pull to the relief of any fisherman whose boat may be swamped. This place is the main drift for fishermen, and this precaution on the part of the Canby crew is wholly voluntary, as they are not required to look after the fishermen. The latter should provide an adequate life-saving station at this point of their own.

June 3, 1893 ADB

Harry Johnson, who was fishing for the Cutting Packing Company in boat *No. 45*, was capsized in the breakers on Clatsop spit yesterday afternoon. He was rescued by the occupants of another fish boat, but his unfortunate boat puller was drowned.

June 3, 1893 ADB

At 2 o'clock this afternoon boat *No. 25* of the Cutting Packing company capsized on the Clatsop spit on the north side of the jetty, half a mile below No. 8 buoy. One of the occupants of the boat was drowned and the other one was rescued by another fishing boat which happened in the vicinity. The life-saving crew came to their assistance and managed to save the boat. It was blowing so hard on the bar at the time that five or six nets had got mixed up together and were drifting toward the end of the jetty and out over the bar. They will be a total loss.

June 3, 1893 ADB

Yesterday afternoon while Peter Nelson, who was fishing for M.J. Kinney, was leisurely sailing his boat up the river past Booth's cannery; he suddenly fell overboard, and before he could be rescued, was drowned. The body was recovered a short time after the accident and taken to Coroner Pohl's undertaking establishment. An inquest was held this morning, and after hearing the testimony, the jury brought in the following verdict: "We, the undersigned jurors, find that the deceased was named Peter Nelson, was about 42 years of age, and a native of Denmark; that he came to his death June 11, 1893, by falling overboard from his fishing boat while intoxicated, opposite Upper Astoria, Oregon, in the Columbia river, and that no one else is to blame for the same."

June 12, 1893 ADB

While the tug *Columbia* was coming up from the bar yesterday afternoon, Capt. Mathews saw a fishing boat drifting onto the edge of Peacock spit. He immediately went to the rescue and was just in time to save the occupants of boat *No. 15*, belonging to J.G. Megler's cannery, from a watery grave, although he did it at the risk of losing the tug, it being necessary to go so close to the spit. The men were very thankful to Capt. Matthews for his timely aid.

June 15, 1893 ADB

Nicholas Vlahutin, a Slavonian, working in the stone quarry at Fisher's landing, was drowned in the Columbia river last Wednesday evening.

July14, 1893 ADB

The Season's Fatalities
Three Fishermen Swept to Sea and Drowned

Now that the close of the fishing season is near at hand and the catch thus far of the gillnet men has been extremely light more and greater chances of going to the bottom of "Davy Jones locker" are taken in an endeavor to even up on a bad season's work by our fishermen. Too many men take too great risks in getting into the breakers at the bar, in the endeavor to get the first of the promised run of salmon which will come with a continuation of warm weather, and not a few of them today owe their lives to the prompt and efficient service of the Canby life-saving crew, who came to their rescue when they had gone beyond the point where they could retreat with safety and gotten into the breakers.

Yesterday morning a heavy fog enveloped the lower river, with a stiff west wind blowing, and a view by the life crew at Canby of the bar was almost totally obstructed until about 10 o'clock when the fog lifted sufficient to reveal five fishing boats bottom up on Clatsop spit. The signal gun boomed and the life boat was manned and started to the rescue in the shortest possible time, in a terrible rough sea. It was found that three men were drowned, one belonging to the Occident Packing Co., and two to the Cutting Packing Co., and their bodies swept to sea. Two of the men known to have been lost were Isaac Backular and his boat puller of boat *No. 11*. As two boats with three men each were picked up, it is thought that at least two other fatalities occurred, but this has not yet been confirmed.

Several fishermen lost their nets owing to the extreme rough weather and several boats are missing. Eleven boats were capsized, but most of them were recovered.

Numerous other mishaps occurred during the day but not as we were informed with fatal results.

The continued presence of the life crew who were out and worked all day accounts for the few fatalities in their location, as they picked up and saved from a watery grave no less than twelve men, and to them great credit is due for the prompt and continued efficient service rendered, and it is but just to them to say that many a fisherman who has fished on the bar this season owes his present lease on life to the strong arms and willing hearts of the Canby life crew who came to their relief at a time when none other was possible. It was rumored that a man fishing for the Scandinavian Packing Co. was among the drowned, but up to a late hour the rumor had not been confirmed. Later reports state that six men were drowned, but up to the hour of going to press their names could not be learned.

July 18, 1893 ADB

The body of Herman Lourilla, the fisherman of the Occident Packing Co. who was drowned on Clatsop spit during the storm of a week ago yesterday, was picked up on Sand island yesterday. Coroner Pohl this morning sent down a coffin, and the deceased was buried at Ilwaco this afternoon.

July 25, 1893 ADB

Coroner Pohl and R.M. Stuart went down to the beach near Gearhart park this morning and exhumed the body of John Rasmussen, a fisherman who was drowned about two months ago and buried the body where found and brought it up this evening for burial at Greenwood.

Aug 8, 1893 ADB

CLOSE OF FISHING SEASON
Over One Hundred Lives Lost This Summer.

The summer fishing season for the year 1893 closed at 12 o'clock last night. Though the catch was behind that of other years, we ought to be satisfied that it was no worse, all things considered.

Ever since the industry was established, it has been conducted with a reckless indifference to its permanent growth and prosperity that has been nothing less than suicidal. The fish have been attacked with a savage greed that has already almost ruined the business. In addition to gill-nets, seines and wheels have been used, and a forest of fish-trap poles in all the bays and on all the shoals has made it well nigh impossible for even a few fish to run the gauntlet and proceed to their spawning grounds.

It is only recently, too, that there was any real attempt to give the fish one free day in the week when they could continue their way up the river unmolested. Well, we are now to pay the penalty of blind, sordid zeal. We have crippled the industry, and should be thankful that the situation is no worse than it is.

But while we consider the commercial and industrial aspects of the business, it is well, too, that we now give some thought to the sentimental and human side. Somehow we have from time to time received the accounts of the disasters to fishing boats in the dangerous region beyond the Desdemona Sands and the consequent loss of life during the season, with little emotion, seemingly accepting these untoward events as a matter of course.

When now, however, we come to look at these calamities in the aggregate and find that one hundred bold and hardy fishermen who sailed down in the beauty of the summer evenings for those perilous fishing grounds and never returned alive, we begin to realize that there is a plaint of breaking and broken hearts in the wail? of the waves that kneel and sob on the low shores of Sand Island.

Only the names of those who belonged to the fishermen's union are known and when their bodies were recovered, they were accorded decent burial. As for the others, who they were or whence they came no one knows. It is only certain that such a number of unknown fishermen were lost, and beyond and before that all is mystery. Somewhere, rude and unlettered as they may have been, there are fond hearts waiting and watching for the coming that death delays and will never know the story of their tragic fate.

Most of the members of the fishermen's union who were drowned, about 60 in all, had families and homes here. Is it not time that something should be done to stay this terrible loss of life in the fishing season?

The government life-station crews have done a noble and heroic work in saving life down at the mouth of the river, but they should not be depended upon entirely.

The cannerymen and the Columbia River Fishermen's Union should join issues and establish a life-saving station of their own at Sand Island by the time another fishing season begins. Such a fearful loss of life as that of the season which has just closed should never occur again.

August 11, 1893 ADB

FRED MITCHELL DROWNED.

Yesterday (Sunday) afternoon about 5 o'clock, Dr. Walker received a brief dispatch from L.N. Mitchell, of Knappa, to come to that place immediately, that his son Fred was drowned, but that he thought there was some hope of restoring life. The doctor at once secured a launch and started for Knappa with all possible speed, but when he reached there, he found that the young man's condition was beyond the reach of medical science or human ingenuity. He was dead, and had been for several hours.

The circumstances of young Mitchell's death is substantially as follows: About 10:30 yesterday morning, in company with a young friend, he went to Knappa slough to go in bathing, and after they had been in the water for about an hour, his companion heard Fred crying for help; and then saw him disappear under the water. It was some time before his body was recovered, but still his parents labored under the impression that there was still life in the lifeless body, but they were hoping against fate. Young Mitchell could not swim, and had waded out to where the water was too deep.

The sad ending of the young man cast a gloom over the entire community where he was well-known and highly esteemed, and the shock was a severe one to his parents, brothers and sisters. He was twenty-one years of age.

August 28, 1893 ADB

Coroner Pohl returned from Knappa last evening, where he had been for the body of Frank Nelson, who was supposed to have been drowned. An inquest was held last evening. The accident was caused by Nelson breaking a blood vessel and falling out of his boat. The deceased was 35 years of age and a single man.

Sept. 19, 1893 ADB

HARRY BANQUIST DROWNED

The Columbia claimed two victims yesterday, the second being Harry Banquist, a fisherman in the employ of the Scandinavian cannery. The accident occurred about 7 o'clock last evening. From what could be learned last night, Banquist had been fishing on the river and was returning home. All went well till the boat arrived off the Scandinavian cannery, when, in attempting to come about, the boat was struck by a heavy squall. The boom swung around so quickly that Banquist had not time to get out of the way, and he was struck a terrific blow on the head, knocking him into the icy water. He was probably rendered unconscious and sank before assistance could reach him. The body has not been recovered. The weather was very rough all day yesterday and the unfortunate man chanced to be a victim. It could not be learned last night whether or not Banquist had a family. He was an old-time fisherman.

Feb. 16, 1894 ADB

Yesterday afternoon, Peter Anderson, who is fishing for the Astoria Packing Company, was on his way home with his little stock of fish, when his boat capsized through the jibbing of his sail. Anderson and his boat puller managed to climb onto the bottom of the upturned boat, but were soon rescued from their perilous position by two brother fishermen.

Apr. 28, 1894 ADB

A boat containing two men was capsized on the spit near the *Republic* wreck on Monday last. A boat pulled to their assistance, but the breakers were rolling too high, and it failed to reach them, and it was with difficulty they saved themselves from being capsized. Both men were drowned.

Pacific Journal, reported in the May 7, 1894 ADB

It was a terror of a night at Sand Island last night, and for several hours, the fishermen down there didn't know whether they were a foot or on horseback. The wind blew and howled, the water roared and splashed, and the gravel flew in every direction, almost pelting the eyes out of the poor fellows who were trying to save life and property. When daylight came, it was found to be necessary to cut adrift from various boats large pieces of nets in order to escape the dangerous tide rips. Tom Quinn's scow was severely damaged, one side being completely blown out... A number of boats were piled high and dry on the island, but no lives were lost. The piles of two condemned traps just below the old wreck of the *Republic* were completely wound round with lost pieces of nets. The only wonder is that no lives were lost.

May 8, 1894 ADB

Quinn was jokingly called the "mayor of Sand Island."

Some fishermen up from down near the bar this morning report that a floater was sighted last night, going out on the ebb tide which was running very fast at the time. It was too near the breakers when noticed to get hold of.

May 12, 1894

Yesterday afternoon boat *No. 47*, fishing for Elmore's cannery, capsized on Peacock spit and the occupants named Jonti and Rovi [Juntti and Rova, perhaps] were rescued by David Laiti, who also fishes for Elmore and who happened to be in the vicinity at the time. The life saving crew at Fort Canby saved the boat and net. Mr. Laiti is making quite a record for himself, he having rescued six *fishemen* from drowning this season.

May 15, 1894 ADB

LOST

The police have the description of a Russian Finn named Peter Kotayarvi, who has been missing since 12 o'clock Saturday night. He was last seen in an intoxicated condition going towards his boat, which was tied to the West Coast cannery, and the supposition is that he was drowned while attempting to get into the boat.

May 23, 1894 DA

CHILD DROWNED

Yesterday evening, as the little 12-year-old daughter of John Lukinen, who fished for the Columbia cannery, was trying to obtain some malt from one of a number of barrels which stand outside of the railing on Hemlock street directly over the river, she leaned too far over, lost her balance, and fell into the water, and was drowned before any one realized the accident. A little boy saw her fall, and instead of reporting it to the Columbia cannery, which was near by, he went home and informed his father, who was at work, but by the time he reached the scene and had inquired if any of the children in the neighborhood was missing, it was too late to save her. The body was found by her father near the place in five feet of water.

May 24, 1894 DA

Yesterday evening, a fisherman, who was drifting abreast of Cathlamet, picked up a neatly finished table which he found floating close by him.

June 6, 1894 ADB

A gentleman who came down from Portland this morning, said that he saw a funny thing in the river yesterday in front of St. Helens. A huge big log came floating along, on one end of which sat a man with his feet curled up under him smoking a pipe, and on the other end sat a large white dog taking observations as cool as a steamboat pilot.

June 6, 1894 ADB

W.D. Smith came down from Vancouver yesterday and exhumed the remains of his son, whose body was picked up on the Washington shores last week. They have been buried by Coroner Pohl at Clatsop. The body will be reinterred at Vancouver today.

June 6, 1894 ADB

George Caboth [Kaboth] met with bad mishap yesterday morning. His fishing house on the seining ground above Tongue Point was washed away by high water and went out over the bar. The loss is considerable.

June 7, 1894 ADB

The body of a man was picked up at Fort Stevens yesterday, and Coroner Pohl notified. The remains were identified as the sailor of the British ship *Holywood*, who was drowned last March. Coroner Pohl buried the body today, according to the instructions from the Captain of the ship.

June 8, 1894 ADB

DAVE BEASLEY DROWNED.
Sinks Beneath the Water Before the Eyes of His Friends.

Dave Beasley, a young man well-known in this city, and who has been fishing with his father since the season opened, met his death this morning by drowning in the channel opposite Kinney's cannery.

It seems that one of Kinney's plungers arrived up from Sand Island about 9 o'clock this morning, and there being insufficient wind to run close in to the cannery, anchor was dropped in the channel, about 200 feet distant from the dock. Sai Get, the Chinese contractor, sent young Beasley out in a skiff for the purpose of bringing in a line from the plunger, with which to pull it to the wharf, and he had just turned back with the line, when Martin Anderson, the plunger's captain, sprang into the frail skiff, which went over like a flash, dumping both men into the turbulent waters. Beasley was considered a remarkably good swimmer, and his friends who saw the accident from the docks felt but little concern, until they saw him making frantic efforts to retain his hold on the upturned skiff. A boat was manned as quickly as possible, but before the rescuers could get to him, he sank beneath the muddy waters and was lost sight of.

In the meantime, Anderson managed to keep afloat until a boat reached him, which was some distance below the scene of the accident. When picked up, he was exhausted.

The deceased was a son of ex-policeman Wm. Beasley, and was aged about 19 years. He was known as an exemplary young man and of great assistance to his father in providing for a large family. The body has not been recovered and it is thought, on account of the swift current in the river, it will never be found.

June 8, 1894 ADB

Last evening when the bar tug came in they reported seeing a boat bottom side up with two men clinging to it, in the choppy water just outside the end of the jetty. It was impossible for the tug to lend any assistance, as the water was too shallow for them to get in. Several fishing boats were seen going to the assistance of the unfortunate fishermen. It is not known whether the men were rescued or not. The boat belonged to either the Hapgood cannery or to the Cutting Packing Co.

June 20, 1894 ADB

TWO BRAVE MEN.

Captain Albert Larsen and boatpuller of Hapgood's boat, *No 13*, did a brave act yesterday which resulted in saving the lives of two fishermen, together with their boat and gear. Yesterday morning, Otto Kaski and boat puller, fishing in Columbia River Packing Co's boat *No. 28*, got into the boiling waters on Desdemona Sands, and before they could clear themselves, their boat went over. They managed to hold on to the upturned boat for some time, but the choppy waves knocked them off several times. Larsen and his boatpuller, who were near when the accident occurred, at once headed for the two unfortunate men, and without hesitation went directly into the dangerous and swirling waters and alongside the capsized boat. It did not take long to get the two men, who were by this time nearly exhausted, into their boat, and without delay secured the boat and net. They took great risk in rescuing the two men, as it was almost impossible for a boat to live in the waters, which were rushing over the sands at the time. The boat and net, together with their owners, were landed at the C.R.P. Co's cannery during the afternoon.

June 20, 1894 ADB

Two fishermen got to skylarking in their boats in front of the city this morning and one of the boats got upset and the contents, including four big salmon, a lunch bucket, and other "ictas," dumped out. They should not play during business hours.

June 21, 1894 ADB

"Ictas" refers to fish; ichthyology is the branch of zoology dealing with fish.

WHISKEY SCOWS.
Most of the Fishermen Favor Driving Them From the River.

There is no possible excuse for whiskey scows. They are nuisances in every sense of the word. They have been more detrimental to many fishermen than any other one thing on the river. That they have been the direct cause of many fisherman finding watery graves goes without saying, and that they have been the indirect cause of murder and plunder, many believe.

More than twenty times this fishing season, the BUDGET has been urged by the better class of fishermen of the Columbia river to advocate the removal of these demoralizing and life destroying arks from the river. Two gentlemen who fish at Sand Island stated to a reporter last evening that a whiskey scow in that locality was the cause of the drowning of Anderson, who fell out of his boat while intoxicated last week. These gentlemen say there will be serious trouble unless the scow moves away from that locality.

Many fishermen who are addicted to drinking bad whiskey spend most of their time and all of their money in these floating man-traps, where they barter their good fish for the vilest kind of rot-gut while their wives and children are at home in need of the actual necessities of life. This is wrong, and steps should at once be taken to expel them from the river. It remains with the fishermen themselves.

June 27, 1894 ADB

Parties are still looking for the body of Young Beasley, who was drowned a short time ago.

June 27, 1894 DA

DAVID BEASLEY.

Olof Turnberg and Chris Schneider, while fishing in Smith's channel, opposite Tanzy point, yesterday forenoon, were startled to see the remains of a man float up against the cork line of their fishing net. They were taken into the boat and brought to the morgue, where they were identified as the remains of David Beasley, son of William Beasley, who lost his life by accidental drowning on the 8th of last month. The body was badly decomposed, almost beyond recognition. The recovery of the remains, however, is a great satisfaction to his parents, brothers and sisters, who have anxiously waited, almost against hope, for him to be found.

A coroner's jury was held on the case today, for what reason the public would like to ascertain, as there was no doubt about the cause of his death.

July 5, 1894 ADB

A NARROW ESCAPE
Eddie Hall had a Close Call From Death
He was Saved by Thoughtful Persons Who Were Near By.

About 2:15 this afternoon while Eddie Hill, the 10 year old son of Mr. and Mrs. George Hill, was playing in a skiff near Kinney's burnt cannery, the skiff capsized and the little fellow went out into the water and after a short struggle went down. Capt. Al. Beard, who heard of the accident rushed to the scene, got a long pole with a hook on the end and pulled the boy out of the water more dead than alive. In fact those who saw him believed that life was extinct. When he was landed, John Ossenberger was thoughtful enough to get a barrel and roll the boy over it for a while, and succeeded no doubt in getting much of the water out of him. After this siege, he was carried to his home, physicians summoned and restoratives applied, and it was not long until Eddie let his anxious parents know that he was worth a good many dead boys. He was in the water about 10 minutes before he was rescued and the wonder is that he was not drowned.

George and Mrs. Hill express their heartfelt thanks to the kind people who so kindly assisted and did all in their power to save their son.

July 19, 1894 ADB

Boat *No. 59*, belonging to Samuel Elmore's cannery, was accidently capsized in the south channel yesterday, midway between Fort Stevens and the end of the jetty. Captain Wilson and his boat puller managed to get hold of the upturned craft and held on until another fishboat came to the rescue. The men were taken aboard, and the greater part of the net was saved by cutting it. The boat and the balance of the net drifted out to *No. 10* buoy, where they were picked up by the Point Adams life crew and turned over to the steamer *Elmore* which happened along at the time on her way in from Tillamook. It is supposed that the two men were intoxicated at the time of the accident and their boat became unmanagable.

July 28, 1894 DA

There was an interesting sight off the waterfront yesterday afternoon, in which two unknown fishermen were the central figures. The tide was just turning and coming in with a heavy current caused by a stiff nor'wester that was blowing at the time. Just off the British ship *Crofton Hall*, the water was very choppy, indicating that it was a shoal place. The fishermen in question, either through ignorance or carelessness, steered directly over the spot, and as a consequence went hard aground. No sooner had they struck than the seas began to go over them, and it was not until they had lowered the sail and had done some vigourous pulling that they got back to the channel. As it was, they were nearly swamped, and the boat had to be baled before the sail could be run up again.

July 28, 1894 DA

August Nelson, while out in a small boat yesterday afternoon, in the vicinity of Booth's cannery, came into rough water and had his boat capsized. Nelson was considered a good swimmer, but while within five yards of the netracks sank beneath the waves and did not again appear. It is supposed that he was seized with cramps.

Nelson was a single man and his relatives here are three brothers and one sister.

July 28, 1894 DA

Narrow Escape

Mr. Nordland, of Hare, left home yesterday morning for Astoria in a small boat to do some trading, and was to have been home in the evening, but on his way back, sometime during the night, his boat was upset and he drifted around until 6 o'clock this morning, when he was picked up by Messrs. Williams and Hellstrom, of Blind Slough. He was on the bottom of his boat, about to give up the ghost when found. He said he had been there for six hours and could not have lasted much longer. Some of Nordland's things were discovered floating in the slough and were fortunately observed by these gentlemen, who took him in and towed his boat to Svensen's Landing.

August 15, 1894 ADB

Several small lads were paddling around this forenoon in an old dilapidated skiff in Scow Bay, when, all of a sudden, the old tub began to sink. They all managed to reach shore but little Willie Elmer, a six-year-old. He went down and would have been drowned only for the timely arrival of Tom Olsen and Peter Hansen, two fishermen, who ran out into the water and carried the little fellow out and took him home.

Sept. 9, 1894 ADB

Last evening Fred Springer arrived here from Mishawaka and reported that Hugh Frazer and Chas. F. Colwell, while coming down the Nehalem river, near the mouth of Rock Creek, ten miles below Mishawaka, had been drowned through their boat striking a rock. Their boat was loaded with lumber to be used for building a cabin for Frazer. Four other persons were on the boat when she struck, but managed to get ashore. Frazer and Colwell were timber locators, and both had cabins on the Nehalem. They were both single men, the former aged about forty-five, and the latter twenty-seven and both were well known around Astoria. It is feared that the bodies will never be recovered as the current is very swift and they no doubt will be swept out into the ocean.

Feb. 26, 1895 DA

Fred Peterson and Geo. Kauri, two fishermen in the employ of the Astoria Packing Co., were capsized off Peacock spit yesterday morning and it was reported both were drowned. It is now learned, however, that Peterson had clung to the boat and was found by the life saving crew floating about on the keel of the boat. He was nearly exhausted and it was several hours before he was resuscitated. The other man perished.

May 9, 1895 ADB

A fisherman who witnessed the capsize of the boat yesterday at Peacock spit, which resulted in the death of one man, George Kauri, and almost drowning of Fred Peterson, severely condemns the life saving crew at Fort Canby for not attending to business. Had they been on the alert, as they are paid to be, these men could have been rescued easily enough. A gun was fired from the cape but the fisherman says it was over two hours before he saw anything of the life saving crew at all. This is surely cause for complaint, particularly this season of the year, when fishing is going on, too much care cannot be taken by these paid watchers. The Budget can give the authority if necessary for this statement.

May 9, 1895 ADB

August Korpela, a Russian Finn fisherman, aged about 50 years, was drowned last evening about 8 o'clock while attempting to reach his scow near the Seaside cannery. Korpela was slightly under the influence of liquor at the time. He had gone ashore for something, and while returning, in some manner, fell from his boat. His partner on the scow, Martin Kulin, heard the splash, and suspecting what had happened, called, asking if it was "Gust." He received an affirmative reply with a frantic request for assistance. There being no boat at the scow, Kulin could do nothing further than to throw a rope to the drowning man. He called to people on shore who immediately responded, but too late to save the man. The body was recovered after about an hour. A doctor was summoned, but he could do no good as the man had been dead nearly two hours when he arrived. Coroner Pohl was notified and took charge of the body. He has not decided whether or not he will hold an investigation.

April 5, 1895 DA

The body of another mutilated man was found floating in mid channel opposite the *Telephone* dock Sunday morning. A boatman brought the body to the city and Coroner Pohl took charge of it. A coroner's jury in the afternoon investigated the affair and Dr. Fulton made an examination of the body. He testified that there were a number of wounds in the head which had been inflicted before the body was put in the water. The jury is still in session, and the body has not yet been absolutely identified. Other witnesses will attend today.

June 9, 1896 DA

A sad accident happened Monday morning by which August Norberg, foreman of the Scandinavian cannery, and Charles Osvik, lost their lives by drowning. It seems that Mr. Norberg was assisting Osvik to moor his boat a short distance east of the cannery. To bring him back after he had moored his boat, Norberg took a very small skiff from a naptha launch. The skiff was scarcely large enough to hold one, let alone two men. It some way it was capsized and both men, neither of whom could swim, were both thrown into the water. Late in the day, the oars from the boat were discovered, which suggested a search, resulting in the finding of both bodies yesterday morning. Mr. Norberg was one of the best known in Astoria and was at one time street commissioner of the city. He was an active member of the fishermen's union, and beside being foreman of the Scandinavian cannery, was also a stock holder in the Alaska Packer's Association. He was a member of the Knights of Pythias and the Seaside Lodge, A.O.U.W. A wife and two children mourn his loss. Charles Osvik was a well known and prosperous fisherman. He was the owner of a ranch on the Nehalem, where his wife is now residing. The funeral of Mr. Norberg will take place Thursday afternoon under the auspices of the orders of which he was a member.

June 10, 1896 DMA

Coroner Pohl yesterday afternoon received word from Clifton that another floater had been discovered near that point, and left on the steamer *Electric* with Sheriff Hare at 4 o'clock to bring the body to Astoria.

June 10, 1896 DMA

Coroner Pohl returned about midnight from Clifton with the body of the man found in the river at that point yesterday. Mr. Pohl says that it is undoubtedly the body of Sam Meilandt, one of the four parties missing from that part of the river last week, among them being the Gunion woman whose body was found a week ago Sunday on the beach at Astoria. The coroner is of the opinion that the body buried yesterday and which was thought by several to have been that of Sam Meilandt, must have been the remains of Gunion, the brother of the woman. Further investigation of the matter will be had today. Several wounds appear on the head of the body brought down last night, apparently made by a sharp instrument.

June 10, 1896 DMA

About 6 o'clock Thursday morning Wood Kerns, Trullinger's light trimmer, fell overboard from Trullinger's wharf into about eighteen feet of water. About the same time Mr. Tom Trullinger awoke and was preparing to dress when he heard the man's cries for help. Suspecting trouble and without waiting to put on his clothes, Mr. Trullinger hurried to the dock and soon found that somebody was in the water. Kearns had in the meantime managed to get hold of one of the piles in the darkness and was holding on for dear life. Mr. Trullinger lowered a boat, and in the darkness, paddled underneath the dock to where Kearns was. When he pulled the man into the boat, he was just about gone, but careful work brought him around during the morning.

Jan. 30, 1897 DA

MORE VICTIMS OF THE COLUMBIA

A lone boat drifting down stream yesterday afternoon with a strong ebb tide, without an occupant, suggested to those on the O.R. and N. dock that perhaps some one was in distress or had been foully dealt with. Investigation proved that in all probability Captain "Charlie" Swanson, of the schooner *Jessie*, had been drowned while attempting to go aboard from his small boat yesterday afternoon.

Sunday afternoon the pilot schooner *Jessie*, in charge of Pilot Malcolm, with Captain Swanson and crew, came into the harbor and anchored just above the O.R. and N. dock in the main channel; it being the schooner *San Jose's* turn to go outside. Yesterday morning at 11 o'clock, the crew were paid off in full, and the captain, according to custom, drew his wages and prepared to return on board as he is the watchman of the vessel while she is in port. At 1 o'clock, he went down to the dock, and started in one of the small boats of the *Jessie* for his vessel. As he passed the *San Jose*, he hailed the captain and asked him to go out with him and look at his trim little ship. The *San Jose's* skipper replied that he could not just then, to which Swanson answered that he would return in half an hour. That was the last heard of Capt. Swanson, as he was soon to go on towards the Jessie.

Only a few minutes after this, the small white boat of the *Jessie* was seen floating down the main channel in a direct line with the *Jessie*, but no one in it. O.R. and N. Watchman Erickson at once lowered his boat and went to capture the runaway. By hard work he succeeded in getting around the dock into the channel and despite the swift ebb tide caught the painter of the *Jessie's* boat and rowed her to the end of the dock. There it was discovered that the runaway boat had no water in her, and that the rowlocks had been taken down and the oars placed on the seats — all ship-shape. An investigating force was at once organized and towed the small boat back to the *Jessie*, where it was soon found that no captain, or watchman was aboard.

When seen last night, Captain Carruthers, owner of the *Jessie*, said that he only knew his skipper and watchman by the name of "Charlie," and could only account for his disappearance upon the theory that after leaving the *San Jose*, he proceeded to the *Jessie*, got alongside, took down his row-locks, placed his oars inside; took the painter in his hand and, in attempting to climb over the rail onto the deck of the *Jessie*, lost his hold by the rolling of the boat in the gale and slipped into the swift current of the river.

"Charlie" Swanson was a well known and popular pilot, having hosts of friends in Astoria. For years he was in the employ of the O.R. and N. Co. on the *San Jose*, and last night Agent Lounsberry said he was one of the most faithful and skillful men they had ever had. His friends are still hopeful that there is some mistake and that he will yet be found somewhere ashore, but up to a late hour no further tidings had been received.

Feb. 16, 1897 DA

THE BODY FOUND

At 8 o'clock yesterday morning, Geo. Beckman discovered the remains of Henry Palmquist, the fisherman who was drowned Monday night on the beach about 100 rods this side of Tongue Point buoy depot.

At the coroner's inquest, held yesterday, after examination of the remains, Dr. J.A. Fulton testified that there were bruises on the head of the deceased, over the eyes and on the left temple. He gave it as his opinion that the bruises were inflicted before death, and that none of them would have caused death, but that death probably was caused by drowning.

Carl Niendorf, another witness, identified the body as that of Palmquist, and stated that he had known the deceased for more than a year, that he was forty six years old, and to the best of his knowledge, was unmarried. He said that he saw him at 3 o'clock Monday afternoon at the Eagle cannery, and that the deceased was then in a perfectly sober condition. Witness stated that about 5:45 p.m. on Monday, he went with the deceased in his boat, both intending to go home, on the other side of Tongue Point, both being perfectly sober. Palmquist steered the boat, and witness was forward, looking after the sail. It was blowing hard, and witness said that Palmquist told him to keep a sharp lookout for the net racks, and let him know in time so as to take down sail. "I was forward when the sail was lowered, and immediately afterwards a squall struck us. He was hauling in the sheet, but the sail jibed, and I heard him hallo twice for help. Before I could get the boom in and get to him, it was too late. I did not see him again. Afterwards, I got help and took the boat around the point to the other side."

George Beckman then testified that he found the remains of Palmquist, whom he recognized, about 8 o'clock yesterday morning, one hundred rods this side of the United States buoy depot at Tongue Point.

After a short deliberation the jury rendered a verdict, finding that Henry Palmquist had come to his death by the boom of his boat striking him and knocking him overboard, causing drowning, on the evening of February 16th.

February 17, 1897 ADB

FISHERMAN DROWNED

Early yesterday morning, John Hendrickson, one of the Columbia Cannery Company's fishermen, was drowned on Clatsop Spit. The boat was turned over in a heavy swell. The boat puller was saved by the fishermen who were near by, but Hendrickson went down before they could reach him. Full particulars have not yet been received. The Fort Stevens life saving crew did all they could to save his life, but could only reach the spot in time to bring the boat puller to shore.

Hendrickson was a Russian Finn, about 35 years old, and leaves no family.

It was also reported that several other boats were capsized in the same swell, and yesterday afternoon, one of Kinney's boats and a net were found capsized on North Shore, but the number of the boat could not be learned, nor were its occupants known up to a late hour. One of the other boats said to be in trouble is supposed to belong to the Cutting Packing Co.

May 1, 1897 ADB

FISHERMAN DROWNED

Another fisherman was drowned yesterday, making the fifth casualty of the season. While sailing off buoy No. 12, Issak Halo, a well known fisherman, who was in the employ of the new fishermen's cannery, was struck on the head by the boom and knocked overboard. The blow rendered the man unconscious and he never came to the surface.

May 25, 1897 DMA

It was reported yesterday that William Lucas, boat puller for Joseph Barnard, fell overboard from his boat yesterday morning near Scarborough Head, and was drowned. No particulars have been learned.

July 27, 1897 DA

Eric Baso, a fisherman, found the body of a man floating in the river opposite the Fishermen's Co-operative cannery this morning. He brought the body to shore and notified Coroner Pohl who took possession of it and buried it this afternoon in the new Clatsop cemetery. The body was hardly in a condition for identification but it answers the description of the man Engwell, of the scow *Hustler* who fell overboard from the Ninth street dock some weeks ago. The only relative that he is known to have had in this vicinity was Louis Ellingson a half brother who works at the Youngs river pulp mill. He has been notified of the finding of the body. There was a reward of $25 offered for the recovery of the body which Baso will be entitled to.

April 15, 1898 ADB

First Drowning Case
Brave Act of Canby Life Crew in Saving One Man

Fort Canby, Wash. May 10 — The first fatal accident of the fishing season occurred about noon today.

Charles Heggblom and Louis Stehlman, fishing for A. Booth & Co. capsized on Peacock Spit. The Fort Canby life saving crew was about one hundred and fifty yards from them when the accident happened and made all possible haste to rescue them, not even waiting to put on their life belts. In doing so the surf boat shipped a heavy sea, which carried it well astern of the fishermen before it could be rounded to. However it was not more than three or four minutes before the crew reached the capsized boat. One of the fishermen, Stehlman, was washed clear of the boat and was seen to go down for the last time before the crew could reach him. The other, Chas. Heggblom, who was foul of the net alongside the boat, was rescued. About forty minutes afterwards the net drifted clear of the breakers, and in picking it up the drowned man was found in it. After working one hour and forty minutes to resuscitate him, it was given up as hopeless. Both men were washed off the boat several times before Stehlman finally became exhausted and sank. The body was taken to Astoria by Fisherman Olof Johnson.

C.D. Stuart, Captain, Fort Canby Life Saving Crew.
May 11, 1898, DA

Coroner Pohl was notified yesterday that the body of a drowned man had been found floating near the Flavel dock. The coroner left on the afternoon train and will return with the body this morning.

May 25, 1898 DA

A Derelict
Old Steamer Hull Found Drifting With Her Sail Set

Last Wednesday, Captain Benson, of the cannery tender *Annie*, belonging to the Pillar Rock Packing Company, found an old scow with an improvised sail set, in the eddy off Jim Crow point says the *Cathlamet Gazette*. He came along side and finding no one on board, took it in tow and anchored it at Pillar Rock. A few days previously John Harrington saw the craft sailing towards Oliver's sands with one man aboard and a skiff towing behind.

The captain of the *Edith* says he noticed on Tuesday last an old man about sixty years old on board. On an examination of the craft it was found that the line which had evidently been made fast to the skiff, had been broken off. From the looks of the tiller it is supposed that the old man had gone into the skiff to repair the lines, leaving the sail set, and a breeze springing up had capsized the skiff, and the old man and his craft are lying at the bottom of the river. The scow had previously been a small steamer and the name "*Carrie*" of Portland is almost obliterated from the stern.

The craft was used formerly to carry wood for some of the steamboats on the Cowlitz river. A few provisions were found aboard the scow and a few personal effects which have been taken care of by Mr. Harrington.

May 28, 1898 ADB

Victor, the 8-year-old son of Victor Rost, the jeweler, was drowned on Saturday evening by falling into the river from the rear of the Central Hotel. He had been fishing in company with little Albert Porter in the basement of the Central Hotel and while Albert left him for a few minutes he disappeared. It was some time before an effort was made to recover his body and when it was brought ashore, life was extinct. From the discoloration around the boy's eyes, it was at first believed that in falling, he had struck his head, but Coroner Pohl could find no marks on it. From laving on his face, the blood settled in and around his eyes. His funeral will take place tomorrow afternoon.

June 6, 1898 ADB

It was reported last evening that one or two fishermen had been drowned near the mouth of the river by their boat capsizing. Inquiry among the cannerymen and fishermen this morning fails to corroborate the story, although all the lower fishing stations have not been heard from.

June 10, 1898 ADB

John Anderson Drowned

At 11 o'clock last night while passing along the net racks at the Co-operative cannery where he had been working on his net, John Anderson fell into the river and was drowned. He was not in the water more than five minutes. Assistance was immediately at hand and the work of resuscitating the unfortunate man was begun, but proved of no avail It is thought he was injured in falling.

Anderson was a resident of Portland where he had lived for a number of years, and was known as an industrious and temperate man. He leaves a family in Portland, his wife now lying confined to her bed with illness. The deceased was a member of Industry lodge, No. 8, A.O.U.W. of Portland. At one time he had charge of the city park in that city.

Since the death of John Hendrickson, who was buried yesterday, Anderson has had charge of his boat and gear. He attended the funeral yesterday and upon his return remarked to some of his companions, "There is no telling, boys, who will be next."

Dr. O.B. Estes, who was summoned and arrived shortly after the body had been taken from the water, states that Anderson was undoubtedly dazed by striking some object in his fall.

June 17, 1898 DA

About three o'clock this morning, Booth's fish boat *No. 2* in charge of M. Roos, capsized near the Peacock spit, with the net out and was drawn into the breakers. Roos and his boat puller got on the bottom of the boat but were washed off several times and were about exhausted when Booth's boat *No. 40*, Captain Christensen, came along and stood clear into the breakers and took them off at the risk of their own lives. The boat and net were subsequently recovered by Stanglund, one of George & Barker's fishermen.

June 28, 1898 ADB

An unfortunate accident happened near Eagle Cliff Sunday evening by which Bessie Waithorp, aged eight years, was drowned. Her father is a fisherman for the Eureka cannery and lives on a scow anchored some distance from the shore. His wife was away on a visit and he went out on the river to make a drift leaving the little girl and her ten-year-old brother on the scow alone. In some way, the little girl fell overboard and her brother jumped after her although he could not swim. He had trouble in getting back to the scow himself but could not bring his sister with him although he had hold of her once. The body was recovered when the father returned from fishing.

June 28, 1898 ADB

James Keating had a very narrow escape from a watery grave yesterday and if a fish boat had not opportunely come along, the Astoria Meat Company would have had a man missing. He had gone down the river in the launch *Star* to meet the incoming ships and in returning over the bar, the machinery of the launch became out of order. The boat drifted hopelessly in the breakers for half an hour and Keating was about ready to make a swim for his life when a fish boat came along and towed the launch out of danger. Launches and Jim will part company in the future.

Sept. 15, 1898 ADB

The three year old son of Matt Furney was drowned yesterday afternoon by falling into the river from the net racks near the Astoria Iron Works. The water was but 5 feet deep and several made immediate efforts to recover the body but it was some time before it could be found and brought ashore. A persistent but unavailing attempt was made to resuscitate it. The funeral will take place tomorrow morning at 10 o'clock from the residence of his parents on Water street. The interment will be in Ocean View cemetery.

Sept. 17, 1898 ADB

There is danger that three Astorians met with a serious accident of some kind yesterday and probably they were drowned. Yesterday morning William Ray, a boiler maker in the employ of the Columbia Iron Works, Knute Thompson, the sailmaker, and another man whose name is not known, borrowed Billy Humble's boat to go fishing down the river for the day. They have not been heard from since in any way and their friends are very much alarmed about them.

Oct. 17, 1898 ADB

Fred Johnson, the milkman, accidently saved the life of a fellow milkman yesterday afternoon while on his way home across Youngs bay. The wind was blowing hard and the water rough at the time, and in addition, it was raining in bucketsfull. He noticed something that looked like an overturned boat but paid no attention to it as he was in trouble himself, until he saw that there was a man on top of it. He then brought his boat about and picked the man up. The man was almost unconscious and could not have held on to the boat much longer. He proved to be Abraham Junna, one of the Young's river milkmen, who was returning home with his milk cans when a squall turned his boat over.

Nov. 23, 1898 ADB

Harry Twilight took an involuntary bath in the river this morning. He was on the train that came down early this morning and after its arrival, it pulled down to the open trestle back of the O.R.& N. dock. It was still dark and he did not notice that the train had shifted its position and stepped off into the river thirty feet below. Fortunately, he struck nothing in his fall and being a good swimmer, was soon able to get out none the worse for the mishap.

Nov. 28, 1898 ADB

Alexander Hanson, a fisherman who lived above Tongue Point, was drowned last evening by the overturning of his skiff near shore opposite Uppertown. He was seen by some men who were on a net rack as he rowed under it when suddenly the skiff turned over and Hanson was thrown in not over three feet of water. He had an oar in his hand but made no effort to wade or swim ashore. He lay on the water with his face down and ropes were thrown across him but he made no attempt to grasp them. A boat was procured and hurried to his assistance, but he was dead, past resuscitation, before he could be got ashore. Coroner Pohl was notified and he took possession of the body and after learning the circumstances decided that an inquest would be unnecessary. Hanson was about 50 years of age and leaves a widow and several children.

Dec. 7, 1898 ADB

The tug *Samson*, with a barge of rock in tow, went down to the mouth of the river this morning with the intention of going to Grays Harbor. The wind was blowing at the rate of 60 miles per hour at the time so she turned back. One of the crew of the *Samson* said that on the bar he could see the waves pick the sand up from the bottom and throw it up in the air.

Jan. 13, 1899 ADB

DROWNED IN YOUNGS BAY

Two young men were drowned within reaching distance of the shore in Youngs bay yesterday afternoon and a third man was rescued by the heroism of Fred Henry who pulled him ashore at the risk of his own life.

The drowned were John Anderson, aged 21, and Rasmus Anderson, aged 18, both large and strong men, being about six feet tall, weighing nearly 200 pounds and strong in young manhood. They were recent arrivals in Astoria, having come here with their mother, who is an invalid, and a sister. They rented a small house by the shore of Youngs bay, near the location of the old oil factory, and it was in sight of it that they were drowned. They were the sole support of the family, and from all accounts were sober, industrious boys, who made a living by cutting wood.

Yesterday morning, they were invited by Hans Jensen, who lived near them, to take a sail up the Walluski. They gladly accepted and started in a little shell of a boat that was hardly capable of holding one, let alone three. They made the up trip in safety and on the return, the wind had sprung up strong from the south west and made quite a swell but skillfully handled she came through the opening in the old Goss trestle and was within a few hundred feet of shore when an effort was made to take the sail down. In doing so, the boat capsized and the three were thrown into the water.

As soon as they came to the surface, they all grabbed the bottom of the boat and foolishly tried to climb on top of it. As they did so, it kept turning over, and they soon became exhausted by their efforts. On shore were a number of people who shouted advice, but there was no boat near by to go to their assistance, so they were compelled to stand by and watch the men drown, except a few boys, assisted by Frank Henry, who got a boat from a Chinaman a quarter of a mile away, and started to row to the scene. Before they could get near, the two young men stopped struggling with the boat, and throwing up their hands, sank out of sight.

At this moment a most exciting and pathetic incident occurred. Jensen was struggling to hold on to the boat when out from the crowd came a little girl about 14 years of age who had an oar in her hands and ran into the water saying: "My papa is drowning. I will save him." By this time the crowd was frantic but Fred Henry who was in the crowd ran into the water and grabbed the girl and brought her back to shore and instructed some men to hold her. He then took the oar and started out after Jensen although he could not swim. After wading out until the water was up to his shoulders, he was able to grasp Jensen and then started back to shore with him.

Jensen was nearly unconscious but grabbed at Henry and if he had not retained his presence of mind, they both would have drowned, although Frank Henry was then close with the boat with two boys straining at the oars. As soon as Fred Henry got Jensen ashore, willing hands were ready to carry him to his home near by and Fred Henry directed his resuscitation. In the meantime, Frank Henry started for town to secure Dr. Estes and on the way notified some fishermen in Uniontown who quickly got some gear together to grapple for the bodies of the two young men.

After a search for a couple of hours, the bodies were recovered almost directly under where they were last seen in the water. Coroner Pohl was notified and took possession of the bodies pending a decision as to whether an inquest should be held but it is unlikely that one will be held as the drowning was witnessed by so many people. The arrangements for their funeral have not yet been made. Some one started the rumor last evening that the three men were intoxicated at the time but this is entirely untrue as they had not had any liquor with them. Their death leaves their mother in distress as she is an invalid confined to her bed.

May 29, 1899 ADB

The increased run of fish that has come into the river during the past few days has caused more gillnet fishermen than usual to venture down close to the bar and there have been many narrow escapes but until yesterday afternoon, when two men lost their lives, no one had been drowned. A strong wind was blowing at the time with a heavy sea running and when Abraham and Oscar Juntti, who were drifting at the edge of the breakers, attempted to put up their sail, their boat was caught by a large swell, thrown onto Peacock spit and capsized. The Canby life saving crew was near at hand and succeeded in saving the boat and net but the men sank before they could be reached. The men live in the lower Nehalem near Ahlers and were fishing for the combine. Their boat bore license number 0822. Earlier in the day another boat contained two men was carried over the bar. The Point Adams life saving crew went to their assistance but owing to the thick weather outside was unable to pick them up and returned in the afternoon. What became of the men is not known. Yesterday was the worst day yet experienced in the lower bay since the season opened. Beside the gale and rough sea running there was a heavy mist that made it impossible to see any distance. There were numerous minor accidents, several nets were lost and that there were not more men drowned is due almost entirely to the vigilance of the Canby and Point Adams life saving crews, both of which followed close to the fishermen during the whole day ready to render assistance.

May 31, 1899 ADB

As Officer Settem was walking his beat in Uppertown at an early hour this morning, he heard cries for help coming from under the roadway near Kopp's brewery. After some difficulty, he secured a boat and rowed to where the cries were coming from. He found a man clinging to a pile and almost exhausted. The man said that he was a sailor from the American bark *Harry Morse* and that in trying to find his way back to the vessel had lost his way and had walked overboard. He said that he had been in the water for several hours before he was rescued.

Sept. 6, 1899 ADB

The disappearance of Louis Love, the *Bailey Gatzert* fireman, is no longer a mystery. The body was found yesterday under the wharf of the Astoria Wood Company and everything indicated that Love had missed his footing in attempting to reach the steamer which lay at the Can Company's dock and fell into the bay. So certain are the authorities that his drowning was purely accidental that no inquest was deemed necessary. The body will be shipped to Vancouver where Love's parents live.

Dec. 8, 1899 MA

A BAD HALF HOUR.
The Dangerous Experience of a County Surveyor.

We often hear people talking about a bad half hour which they have spent at some period of their lives, and who has not passed one at some time, remarks the *Skamokawa Eagle*, but few are fated to pass a more dangerous half hour than did Richard Strait, county surveyor of Wahkiakum county, one day last week.

Mr. Strait was on his way from Skamokawa to Grays River. He was sailing before a squally East wind, there was considerable sea running and the boat rolled down, the foot of the sail caught under water and the boat, which was small and heavily ballasted, swamped and sank stern first. He climbed up the boat's mast as it went down and at last, pushed out of sight under the water, the boat sinking in seven fathoms. Then commenced a struggle for life.

He was then opposite Chris K. Henry's place and the tide was ebbing quite fast, the water was icy cold and he was weighted down with heavy clothes. He knew he could not make the shore at Henry's so he struck out with the current for Elliott's point, keeping well clear of the eddies. Arriving off Elliott's, the current took him off shore, but here his cries for help attracted the attention of the people on shore and a boat put off to his assistance.

He was well nigh exhausted when George Elliott pulled him into his boat and took him ashore, but he met with the kindest of treatment from the people of Elliott's landing and by next morning, he had recovered sufficiently to resume his journey. He lost his boat and gear but fortunately his valuable surveying outfit was not in the boat at the time of the accident.

Dec. 16, 1899 DMA